POLITICAL THEORY AND
POLITICAL EDUCATION

POLITICAL THEORY
AND
POLITICAL EDUCATION

EDITED BY MELVIN RICHTER

PRINCETON UNIVERSITY PRESS
PRINCETON, NEW JERSEY

Published by Princeton University Press, Princeton, New Jersey
In the United Kingdom: Princeton University Press, Guildford, Surrey

Library of Congress Cataloging in Publication Data will be
found on the last printed page of this book

Publication of this book has been aided by the Whitney
Darrow Publication Reserve Fund of Princeton University Press

Clothbound editions of Princeton University Press books
are printed on acid-free paper, and binding materials are
chosen for strength and durability.

Printed in the United States of America by Princeton
University Press, Princeton, New Jersey

CONTENTS

NOTES ON CONTRIBUTORS

Allan Bloom is Professor of Social Thought in the Committee on Social Thought and the College, at the University of Chicago. He has translated, with an interpretative essay, Plato's *Republic* (N.Y.: Basic Books, 1968).

Ronald Dworkin is University Professor of Jurisprudence, Oxford University, and the author of *Taking Rights Seriously* (Cambridge, Mass.: Harvard University Press, 1977).

Mihailo Marković is Professor of Philosophy, University of Belgrade, a member of the Serbian Academy of Arts and Sciences, and the author of *From Affluence to Praxis: Philosophy and Social Criticism* (Ann Arbor: University of Michigan Press, 1974).

J.G.A. Pocock is Professor of History, The Johns Hopkins University, and author of *The Machiavellian Moment* (Princeton: Princeton University Press, 1975).

Melvin Richter is Professor of Political Science, City University of New York Graduate School and Hunter College. He has translated, with an interpretative essay, *The Political Theory of Montesquieu* (New York and Cambridge: Cambridge University Press, 1977).

Charles Taylor is Chichele Professor of Social and Political Theory, Oxford University, and the author of *Hegel* (New York and Cambridge: Cambridge University Press, 1975).

Michael Walzer is Professor of Government, Harvard University, and the author of *Just and Unjust Wars* (New York: Basic Books, 1977).

Bernard Williams is Provost of King's College, Cambridge University, and author of *Descartes: The Project of Pure Enquiry* (New York: Viking, 1978; Harmondsworth: Penguin Books, 1978).

Sheldon Wolin is Professor of Politics, Princeton University, and the author of *Politics and Vision* (Boston: Little, Brown and Co., 1960).

PREFACE

This book is the result of an international meeting of the Conference for the Study of Political Thought, made possible by grants from the Humanities Division of the Rockefeller Foundation and from Dr. Harold Proshansky, President of the City University of New York Graduate School and University Center, where the Conference met. Thanks are due to both the Rockefeller Foundation and to President Proshansky from the Conference and the Editor.

The Conference for the Study of Political Thought is an interdisciplinary organization composed of many discussion groups throughout Canada, the United States, and Australia. The Conference has held international meetings since 1969, and publishes a newsletter, edited at the University of Missouri, Kansas City, by Professor Lyman Tower Sargent. At the time of writing, its officers are J.G.A. Pocock, The Johns Hopkins University; Nannerl Keohane, Stanford University; and R. A. Fenn, Department of Political Economy, University of Toronto, Toronto, Canada, from whom information about membership may be obtained.

The Assistant Director of the Princeton University Press, Mr. Sanford Thatcher, has been most helpful throughout the publication of this volume, as has Dr. Susan Tenenbaum, who assisted in organizing the conference's international meeting, and in preparing this book. My principal indebtedness is to my wife, Michaela Wenninger-Richter, for her encouragement and editorial assistance, and above all, for her numerous and valuable suggestions about how to shape the introduction.

Melvin Richter
INSTITUTE FOR ADVANCED STUDY
PRINCETON, NEW JERSEY

POLITICAL THEORY AND
POLITICAL EDUCATION

EDITOR'S INTRODUCTION

MELVIN RICHTER

This book is a collection of previously unpublished papers by prominent political theorists working in a number of disciplines and styles. The purpose of the introduction is to make the papers more useful both for readers who may be familiar with one sort of theory and not another, and for those beginning work in political theory and its history. The introduction therefore presupposes little more than a general interest in these subjects. Although the contributors have had the opportunity to comment on the introduction, responsibility for it belongs to the editor alone.

This introduction will survey some of the changes that have occurred in political theory, but for the most part it will sketch the background of the issues discussed by the contributors, relate their papers to what they have written elsewhere, and identify both the convergences and the unresolved differences among them.

This volume both acknowledges what political theorists have achieved in the past decade and points to problems that need to be discussed in the future. Some papers ask how the varied approaches used by professional practitioners of political theory have illuminated significant questions; others explore ways in which to extend political theory to problems confronting citizens and their government.

The publication of this volume is meant to open a discussion that could not even have been contemplated twenty-five years ago. At that time many social scientists and philosophers believed that political theory and its history had nothing to contribute to their respective subjects. That situation has been altered.

There is no uncontested definition of political theory. Both politics and theory are abstract terms. Their use has always varied with the epistemology, ethics, philosophical method, political interests, and social location of the theorist. In any case, as several papers in this volume argue, the fact that a political term is contested or inherently contestable need not deter us from using it. "Political theory" will be used here to include the subjects of moral and political philosophy and their histories. So understood, the term does not exclude classifications, descriptions, or explanations of political arrangements and action.

This usage follows from a distinction made by many contributors. They emphasize the difference between theories formulated from the point of view of a political agent—whether citizen or statesman—oriented to action, and theories that assume the position of a neutral, scientific observer concerned only to generalize about the behavior of others. It is from this standpoint that behavioralist social scientists and positivist philosophers have distinguished empirical from normative theory, facts from values, and descriptive from prescriptive propositions. These classifications are rejected by the contributors to this volume. They regard this terminology as deriving from logical empiricism or logical positivism in general philosophy and from non-naturalism in moral philosophy. The status of these philosophical positions is dubious, and to import them as methodological canons for political theory would require justifications rather stronger than those thus far produced.

The concept of political education also is open to disagreement. No attempt will be made here to paper over differences or to stipulate some neutral or synthetic meaning. In many classical Greek or Roman theorists, the notion of political education is hard to distinguish from that of indoctrination. Both rulers and ruled, it was thought, ought to be trained in whatever knowledge, beliefs, and behavior that might be demonstrably necessary to establish and maintain a given regime. Such education would vary, depending on whether the regime were the best form, the best attainable in the circumstances, or simply that which exists. Rulers may have to be trained altogether differently from subjects, or the nature of the political order may dictate an essentially similar education.

Political education, if so reduced to indoctrination, is incompatible with most modern theories of democracy and their moral and political vocabularies. But political theorists have not as yet contributed enough to this subject. Its consideration by them is surely desirable. Three papers in this volume do discuss political education. Michael Walzer advocates developing a discipline that teaches the practical application of general moral and political principles. He believes that both citizens and office-holders ought to learn how to take into account their principles of right and wrong when making political decisions. For Sheldon Wolin, the consequence of having untheoretical political commentators is that they educate the public to perceive politics as non-problematical. What needs to be done is to train commentators who, through a vision of politics derived from theory, can aid citizens both to perceive alternatives to existing arrangements and to arrive at the models of a better society. Ronald Dworkin considers the relationship between legal and political education. When he proposes that political philosophers work out the meaning of such principles as equality so that judges can apply them in crucial cases, he recalls one of the oldest conceptions of the relationship in which theorists should stand to politics.

This volume contains still another application of political education. Most political theorists now are university teachers. Yet the training they give their students still is largely determined without systematic consideration of the full range of existing alternatives. To state them and to consider their respective claims to be included in the training of political theorists was among the aims of the conference from which these papers derive. Thus the papers on political theory are concerned, as Allan Bloom remarks, with how the next generation of professors ought to be trained. The contributors to this section addressed themselves primarily to specifying the contributions made by their own way of doing political theory and its history. Thus the knowledge and the teaching (or *paideia*) of political theory on the one side; and political education, on the other, are the central concerns of this book.

In the 1950s political theory in the strong sense was thought to be on the verge of extinction.[1] The reasons for this diagnosis of imminent decease given by social scientists and philosophers did not altogether correspond, perhaps because communication between them was minimal. Yet such disagreement was all the more surprising because social scientists had achieved their emancipation from philosophy by adopting one of its forms. Logical positivism was the basis of the methodology that became canonical for empirical inquiry. Among its tenets were the verification theory of meaning, the assertion that all normative judgments are arbitrary, and the adoption of a program for making the study of politics into a natural science of behavior. The practitioners of this new science would be neutral as to their findings. Their goal was to formulate a body of theory that could be tested by empirical investigation. Such theory would be intersubjectively verifiable and hence incontestable; its purpose would be to explain and predict behavior. Political systems, thus viewed, are epiphenomenal—explicable, that is, only by relationship to the larger social system of which they are one part. The brute data for such study were to be obtained by inquiry into the correlations between units of analysis logically definable as separate from one another.

Those accepting such a program viewed the history of political science and sociology as precisely analogous to the pre-modern history of the physical sciences. Both are records of mistakes. Not the least of the errors in the past study of politics had been to take seriously philosophical discussions of the ideal ends of politics. It became widely accepted that realism was the appropriate attitude for those investigating political behavior, particularly in international politics. Previous failure to achieve scientific theory in that field, according to these theorists, was the result of the moralism and idealism of its practitioners. They had been infected by the incorrigible and inherent defects of political philosophy. This produces either fanaticism or unacceptable unanticipated consequences. Thus, to talk about rights, or such principles as justice, liberty, and equality is to be ideological and unscientific. To the extent that it is possible to maximize welfare, this is best done by the calculating and compromising set of attitudes requisite to the bargaining and interest aggregation of democratic political systems.

From social scientists with such a perspective came the prediction of the end of ideology in modern industrial societies. The immanent characteristics of such societies were said to be rationality, science, organization, technological progress, and general material prosperity. These trends would lead to the liquidation of those general belief systems known as ideologies that have in the past produced the excesses of political fanaticism.

Although seldom formulated as such, the death of political philosophy was perceived as one part of the end of ideology. "Normative political theory" was considered by social scientists to be impossible in principle. And its history was simply an antiquarian enterprise in the eyes of those concerned to get on with the new science of politics. Thus for them the death of political philosophy and its history were not to be regretted.

At about the same time, philosophy in the English-speaking world was dominated by the work of Wittgenstein, Austin, Ryle, Hare, and Stevenson. None of these had much interest in politics, nor did their work encourage philosophers to do political theory. Yet analytical philosophy was being transformed by developments that seemed at the time to be of purely technical interest, such as the explanation of human action and moral theory.

Those concerned with those subjects were to help supersede what had been the single most important book for English-speaking philosophers, A. J. Ayer's adaptation of logical positivism in his *Language, Truth, and Logic* (2nd ed. with new preface, 1946). Arguing from a three-fold division of judgments into logical, factual, and emotive, he concluded that verifiability is the criterion of what is meaningful in judgments other than those purely analytical in character, i.e. logic and mathematics. Because it is impossible to confirm or disconfirm moral judgments, they are not really judgments at all. Although a moral judgment appears to be a meaningful sentence, it in fact expresses only purely personal attitudes. Ayer thus stresses the subjectivity of morality, a view that applies as well to political judgments.

Another much-read ethical theorist at this time was C. L. Stevenson, who emphasized the effects of emotive language. The essence of moral discourse, he argued in *Ethics and Language* (1944), is the speaker's effort to affect people's feelings or attitudes and hence their behavior. Moral language thus is used to persuade others to favor or to do what we do. Such terms produce emotional reactions, either through associations with past usage, or through persuasive definitions.

Emotivism, as this position was called, then was followed by the prescriptivism of such philosophers as R. M. Hare. In *The Language of Morals* (1952) and *Freedom and Reason* (1963), Hare argued that the essence of moral discourse is not influence but guidance. Moral utterances are a species of prescriptive discourse that closely resemble imperatives. In short, moral utterances tell you to *do* something: Their distinctive quality is not what the emotivists argued it to be, namely to *get* you to do something. In addition, a moral judgment, in Hare's view, not only entails an imperative, but also is universalizable. That is, such a judgment logically commits the agent to making similar judgments about any similar situation.

Prescriptivism differed from emotivism in that it did not represent moral discourse as non-rational. Yet, philosophers such as Hare continued to assert that moral statements cannot be deduced from any statement of fact and that we are free from the point of view of logic or language to apply prescriptive terms to whatever we may wish to commend or condemn. If asked to provide reasons for a moral view, a speaker may refer to the facts of the case in question or to the principles applied in the judgment. Thus to give reasons is to refer to one's own prescriptions. This is to say nothing about their rightness except that they are consistent. In case of disagreement, there are no reasons independent of the speaker, whose principles are whatever they may happen to be.

In one of the few philosophical books read by social scientists in the 1950s and 1960s, T. D. Weldon adapted Hare's metaethical prescriptivism to political theory. Just as Hare had discussed not the substantive issues of morality but its language and logic, so Weldon's subject was not the substantive issues of politics, but as his book's title stated, *The Vocabulary of Politics*.[2] In this view, judgments in morals and politics derive from deductive inferences. Their premises are the result of pure choice. On this account, moral and political theorists cannot make substantive contributions to their subjects. Nor can they discuss meaningfully political goals, ends, purposes, or principles. Thus Hare and Weldon were non-naturalistic in their emphasis upon facts; they claimed to be non-normative when they discussed the logic or language of ethical or political discourse; and they assumed that any judgment of value is based upon a choice that has no reason or ground independent of the person making it.

Thus far analytical philosophers and social scientists were in agreement. However the philosophers then began to give up verificationism. The process was complex, but may be briefly characterized in noting Wittgenstein's movement from the theory of meaning he had presented in his *Tractatus Logico-Philosophicus* (1921) to that developed in his later philosophy, particularly in his lectures published posthumously as *Philosophical Investigations* (1953). The *Tractatus* presented the theory that for a sentence to have meaning, it must picture a fact. This restriction of meaning became the program of the Vienna School of logical positivism. Applying Wittgenstein's notion to sense experiences, this school developed the verificationist doctrine that for a sentence to have meaning is to correlate it to a type of experience that makes it true. All knowledge of fact must be derived from observation. Thus science and mathematics were regarded as the model for human rationality, and any other form of discourse as meaningless.

Wittgenstein came to reject his first position. He came to see meaning not as the correlation between sentences and sense experience, but as the use of words within the context of all those varied circumstances within which they are used. Thus Wittgenstein later emphasized the great variety of ways in which language may be employed in public conditions. This concern for what people actually do with language and language games came to replace the search for one strict theory of meaning derived from mathematics and the physical sciences. In addition, the verification principle ran into technical difficulties that led many philosophers to conclude that it could not be formulated satisfactorily in the way that positivists wanted it to be. Finally, philosophers came to believe that it was impossible to accept the implications of positivism for ordinary statements about material things and for judgments of value.

At about this same time, in the early 1960s, philosophers began to investigate human action and its explanation. Out of their attention to what is entailed by the language we use to describe and explain how humans behave came a critique of positivism that made possible changes in moral, legal, and (at a later stage) political philosophy. Such considerations led to taking seriously concepts such as intention, purpose, and giving reasons. In the philosophy of law, these notions could be used to investigate such questions as responsibility and fault. They could be used to criticize the ethical theory of Ayer, Stevenson, and Hare:

> When I say, 'You ought to do this,' or when I say, 'This is good,' I want to protest that I say more and other than 'You or anyone—do this!' or, 'I like this. Do so as well.'

For if this is what I mean, that is what I could and would say. . . . But when I invoke such words as *ought* or *good* I at least seek to appeal to a standard which has other and more authority. If I use these words to you I seek to appeal to you in the name of these standards and not in my own name.[3]

Thus moral sentences using moral language entail giving reasons. Their grammar precludes simple assertion of arbitrary preference.

As late as 1966, analytical philosophers, despite their interest in the theory of action, still did not devote much attention to political philosophy. In a volume edited for European readers, Alan Montefiore and Bernard Williams made this point.[4] They explained such lack of interest in part by the stability of British political experience, and in part by the sober professionalism of analytical philosophers, who chose to address themselves to problems and puzzles of interest to colleagues and students. Montefiore and Williams contrasted the deliberate choice of everyday usage to the emphasis on extreme situations, often political, among European existentialists. In a paper printed in their book, Richard Wollheim asked whether there was anything about the analytical style that made it impossible to write political philosophy. Although like his editors, Wollheim denied that this was the case, he nevertheless conceded that since the dominance of the analytical idiom, no major work of political philosophy had appeared.

The political crises of the 1960s provided the occasion for political theorists to apply the theoretical instruments recently sharpened by the philosophers. In his paper written for this volume, Bernard Williams makes the point in a way that raises significant issues:

. . . living political philosophy arises only in a context of political urgency, and the somnolence of political philosophy was to that extent a phenomenon of the period that prematurely saluted the end of ideology. . . . For political philosophy's habitual, and it seems, ineliminable dependence on the urgency of political questions, which are not in the first place philosophical, is of a piece with its insistence, when at all interesting, in being both normative and impure.

Yet, it would seem, urgency is not enough. Those who would alter a subject must be technically prepared. Crisis may be a necessary, without being a sufficient, condition. This may have been the case with many social scientists in the late 1960s who attacked the assumptions and methods of their discipline. An alternative mode of carrying on a subject must be available, as well as a series of practical occasions for its application.

These interactions are most obvious in the United States. The civil rights movement led first to the discussion of civil disobedience, and then to the moral dimensions involved in turning formal rights into practical reality. The War on Poverty, so-called, of the Johnson Administration raised questions, not only of the equity of existing arrangements, but of further issues as well: How ought the concept of justice to be phrased? What is its relationship to liberty, equality, and property?

The American involvement in Vietnam made it necessary to think about difficult theoretical problems: the legality of the war, the legitimacy of a government that carried it on so brutally, the principles that would or would not justify individuals in resisting or not complying with orders of that government. At the same time, many gave serious consideration to communitarian and participatory ideals for the society as a whole, or for groups who chose to live so. Black militants caused others as well to ask whether the basis of American society was racist, and if so, whether compensatory reverse discrimination is moral and constitutional. The women's movement raised similar issues not only about discrimination, but also about domination on the basis of sex. Finally, the Watergate scandal, as well as revealing illegal actions taken by the FBI and CIA, created concern about the absence of moral and political principle in the actual conduct of moral and political life.

Many of these themes were at the center of books which, in the 1970s, registered a great change in the status of political theory. Upon the appearance of John Rawls's *A Theory of Justice* (1971), reviewers commented that at last there was one major work worthy of close reading and criticism. One such appreciation appeared in a book of a disparate political orientation, also cited by Bernard Williams as a work of major significance, Robert Nozick's *Anarchy, State, and Society* (1974). Despite Nozick's disagreement with Rawls's concept of justice, he writes: "It is a fountain of illuminating ideas, integrated into a lovely whole. Political philosophers must now work within Rawls's theory, or explain why not." There is now an increasing number of books focusing on first-order principles. Even their critics concede that they merit detailed attention of a sort not given to political theorists a decade ago. Several contributors to this volume recently have published major books that may turn out to be of the same order of significance as those by Rawls and Nozick.

The history of political theory has shared in the general upturn of the 1970s. Any reawakening of interest in political philosophy may be counted on to provide new perspectives on the past. Because of their quality, great political philosophers have always provided a major stimulus to later theorists. These in turn tend to redefine their relationship to past great philosophers in terms of their own concerns and methods. A number of historians of political theory have made novel uses of the concern with language that has characterized analytical philosophy. One historical work by a political philosopher with such training is Alasdair MacIntyre's *A Short History of Ethics*. He insists that a historical dimension is needed to correct truncated and incomplete notions of what can and cannot be thought, said, and done. Such a dimension makes it possible to specify the relationship between moral and political argument on the one side, and forms of social life on the other.

Another use of analytical philosophy by historians of political theory has come through those who emphasize the importance of conceptual vocabularies to political thinkers. They derive their definitions of their situation, of alternatives to it, and of their standards of legitimacy from such categories. Thus their effects upon action can be studied by attention to changes in the vocabulary over time. Perhaps the leading example of this program thus far realized is J.G.A. Pocock's *Machiavellian Moment*, which will be discussed in its relation to his paper in this volume.[5]

It would be misleading to suggest that interest in the history of political theory has been sustained only by developments in analytical philosophy or by the political crises of the 1960s. Many groups and individuals have been prompted by quite different influences. Among them is the large number of those whose guide has been the late Professor Leo Strauss, who did so much to keep alive political philosophy during the period when behavioralism might have driven it out of the social sciences. Professor Michael Oakeshott and his students have played a similar role in Great Britain. Another significant group has been that which formed at Berkeley around Sheldon Wolin, John Schaar, Norman Jacobson, and Hanna Pitkin. Other scholars have worked along the lines of their training at major graduate schools by C. H. McIlwain, George H. Sabine, Carl J. Friedrich, and Franz Neumann. Finally no account of recent political theory and its history ought to omit mention of the late Hannah Arendt. Her work had little to do with philosophy written in English, yet she stimulated many by her originality and commitment.

By the late 1970s political theory had become among the most popular subjects in departments of political science and philosophy. From 1975 to 1978, the largest attendance in any field at American Political Science Association annual meetings was in political theory and its history. Philosophers have demonstrated a corresponding interest. No fewer than four journals have been founded since 1971: *Philosophy and Public*

Affairs (1971), *Interpretation* (1971), Political Theory (1973), and the *Canadian Journal of Political and Social Theory* (1977). These newer publications join the two valuable series that have appeared throughout the period under discussion: *Philosophy, Politics and Society* in Great Britain, and *Nomos* in the United States. The Conference for the Study of Political Thought, a North American organization with many branches throughout Canada, the United States, and Australia, was formed in 1967. These groups provide a meeting point for those working in political theory, whatever their departmental affiliation. The Conference also holds annual international meetings on particular problems in political theory and its history.

The remarks that follow are intended to sketch in the background for the essays printed in this book. Each will be treated both in relationship to other work done by the author and in terms of its general implications. It is not easy to strike the proper balance between claiming too much for these essays and missing their significance altogether. This introduction registers the editor's experience, at once exhilarating and sobering, of attempting to take in and assess the bewildering variety and richness of what is now being done by political theorists. Even so, it turned out to be impossible to include certain important approaches, such as attempts to apply economic models and decision theory to politics and society; critical theory and phenomenology; and, in the history of political theory; efforts to relate ideas to their social and economic context, and the contrasting approach that views theory as part of traditions of behavior. No doubt such omissions will be harshly judged in some quarters. This is to be expected, as is the discrepancy between what will be concluded about such variety as there is. What some will take as evidence of creativity, others will find to be confusion. These essays are written from varying points of view. What they share is the rejection of logical positivism and the positions resting upon it.

Political theorists are still in a transitional phase. From being always and everywhere on the defensive, they are now moving increasingly to their own positive work. But there is a dialectic connected with transition. Many of these essays begin with a sketch of two alternative models: the first some version of a rejected orthodoxy; the other embodying the principles and method of its author. Such an exposition often involves turning the tables on those who regard themselves as speaking from the most advanced positions of science, enlightenment, or emancipation. This strategy can mean designating realism as itself a moral position, or logical positivism as the unwarranted imposition of an exclusively philosophical standard upon activities essentially practical in nature. Some authors argue that any claim to neutrality is based on a less than scientific awareness of the observer's actual position. Others argue that theorists who pride themselves on their technical capacity to handle even the most complex decisions do so only by being simple-minded, by "having too few thoughts and feelings to match the world as it really is."[6] Finally, such a mode of argument can mean identifying as the chief obstacle to progress precisely those parties or intellectual movements that define themselves as progressive.

Taken together, these essays cannot be regarded as presenting unanimous recommendations derived from common premises and an agreed method. Some of them dissent explicitly from all the others. Some refrain from voicing disagreement in order to get on with the author's own argument. The contributors were chosen to represent diverse approaches to their part of the subject. At the conference that was the occasion of these essays, this was the assignment for those who proposed to treat the potential contributions of their method to the training of future political theorists. The papers given by Michael Walzer and Sheldon Wolin were written for comment by persons outside university life engaged in activities to which political theory might be applicable. Ronald Dworkin's essay turned out to have the same thrust in its treatment of judges and jurisprudence.

Bernard Williams's subtle analysis of the relationship between analytical philosophy and political theory needs no clarification. So succinct is its statement of a complex relationship that what is most wanted is not so much explication as exemplification, particularly for those lapidary remarks dismissing utilitarianism. Until recently, most analytical philosophers believed that utilitarianism provided the most satisfactory way of working out moral and political theory. Many no longer think so, and the reasons for this change are in part to be found in the instruments used in this attack upon it. It may be instructive to see how Williams makes his case against utilitarianism. He does not do so in the same way as Alasdair MacIntyre, who makes a similar judgment:

> Eighteenth-century English moralists and nineteenth-century utilitarians write from within a society in which individualism has conquered. Hence they present the social order not as a framework within which the individual has to live out his moral life, but as the mere sum of individual wills and interests. A crude moral psychology makes of moral rules instructions as to effective means for gaining the ends of private satisfaction.[7]

Williams does not use this sociological analysis. Nor does he resort to the history of the subject of self in modern epistemology as does Charles Taylor in his work on Hegel.[8] Finally, he does not rest his case upon a theory of rights, as do Dworkin and Walzer in their most recent books.

For Williams, the adequacy of utilitarianism as a moral theory is to be judged on the basis of the account it gives of human personality, actions, intentions, and integrity. Utilitarianism is a distinctive way of looking at human action and morality. The issue for Williams is not so much whether one agrees with utilitarianism's answers. Rather the most significant question is whether its way of putting things is acceptable. Williams finds that utilitarians cannot coherently give an account of the relation between a person's projects, desires, and actions.

As a moral theory, utilitarianism has implications for politics. This is because utilitarianism is a form of consequentialism, "the doctrine that the moral value of any action always lies in its consequences, and that it is by reference to their consequences that actions, and indeed such things as institutions, laws, and practices are to be justified if they are to be justified at all."[9] Williams holds that this excludes the possibility of there being some situations in which it would be right to do an action even though the state of affairs it might produce would be worse than others available. Utilitarianism cannot rule out any available course of action. Indeed, tough-mindedness is a utilitarian virtue, and squeamishness is treated as the self-indulgent or cowardly refusal to follow out the logical implications of one's thoughts.

People who do not absolutely rule out any action are prepared to think about extreme situations in which they could justify doing what ordinarily they would not do. Once they have begun thinking in this way, the differences between extreme situations and less extreme ones come to be perceived as no longer the difference between the extreme and the usual, but between the greater and the less. Thus consequentialist morality in general, and utilitarianism in particular, tends to produce attitudes that brutalize at the same time that they make actors proud of their self-sufficiency. "Making the best of a bad job is one of its maxims, and it will have something to say even on the difference between massacring seven million and massacring seven million and one."[10]

Williams is opposed to this so-called realism, as is Michael Walzer in his book on just and unjust wars.[11] It produces a certain kind of fantasy on the part of those educated to glory in their toughness. It fails to recognize that unless the environment has a minimum degree of sanity, "it is insanity to carry the decorum of sanity into it."[12] Thus, consequentialism tends to make the agent accept all situations as qualitatively similar. It discourages anyone from refusing to accept a situation that is morally impossible.

Utilitarianism also can be used as a system of political and social decision. Williams points out how it is used as the criterion and basis for judgment by legislators and administrators on the one side, and as a system of private morality on the other. Either citizens will themselves use utilitarian criteria, or they will not. If citizens are utilitarians, they will expect their government to be so as well. In that case there will be no concern with justice or equity. If, on the other hand, the government is utilitarian, but citizens are to a significant degree, non-utilitarian, then the government must use manipulative techniques. For either the government does not respond to non-utilitarian demands, or else it will have nothing to respond to because the citizens' non-utilitarian preferences will be directed purely to private objects. This can happen only if the government makes it so. The situation will look very different to the ruling elite and to the ruled. Hence, utilitarianism will always create the possibility of manipulation because it is so conscious of handling situations by altering the attitudes of the population. Indeed utilitarianism encourages an elite to do whatever it regards as most productive of general utility. Principles of morality are here superfluous. And indeed the elite is led to believe that the calculations requisite for general utility can be made only by those trained as the elite has been.

Utilitarianism is apt to produce a particular kind of political education. It teaches not only tough-mindedness and the inconsequence of moral principle, but also cynical manipulation. As a moral and political theory, it is alarmingly good at combining technical complexity with simple-mindedness. In terms of its effects upon public officials, it must be ranked as among the worst types of political education in a democracy.

In his contribution to this book, Charles Taylor argues that political theorists ought to know the distinctive philosophy of science used by most social scientists and the theoretical alternatives to it. Theorists should be able to discuss the full range of conceptual languages that may be applied to politics. Only in this way can they point out those dimensions of politics that cannot be dealt with by the behavioralist method. If they are to influence their colleagues, they also must develop another way of studying politics that will combine description and prescription within a vocabulary that can handle both.

Among the most novel elements of Taylor's analysis is his presentation of the way behavioralist social scientists view themselves, their philosophy of science, and the criticisms made of it. He explains that those using the dominant positivist method are not unaware of many issues that, strictly speaking, cannot be located on their conceptual grid. What happens is that they make an approximate translation into their own language. In the eyes of their critics, this translation may be unsuccessful, but in the view of those performing such an operation, they have been incorrectly accused of having ignored such issues as whether they can set aside their personal values while studying politics. Taylor's contribution here is to identify the philosophical differences among the conceptual vocabularies in question.

Much of Taylor's previous work helped prepare him for applying to the social sciences those sophisticated tools he had acquired as an analytical philosopher. The important book he has since published on Hegel contains a striking history of the study of man that emerged, first as part of the early modern scientific revolution, and then as a reaction against it. Taylor goes on to evaluate the frameworks and concepts that emerged from both movements. At the center of his analysis are their implications for political theory and practice.[13]

In his first book, *The Explanation of Behaviour*, Taylor contrasted those mechanistic explanations provided by behavioral psychologists with the teleological explanations found in the analytical theory of action.[14] This theory stresses human goals, purposes, or intentions. Against them, the behavioral psychologists held, as did logical positivists of the Vienna School, that reductionism is essential to science. The real world, or language, or knowledge (depending upon the interest of the theorist) consists of a complex made up of simpler and more basic elements. The task of science is to reduce the complex and unanalyzed into its simple components. Nothing significant about human behavior is omitted by such a reduction: Indeed, this operation is essential to any true science. If a science of behavior is to be achieved, it must produce basic postulates, from which complex theorems are developed. These theorems can be tested by experimental evidence. And from such a system would be derived further predictions.

The greatest obstacle to such a science of behavior, in the eyes of behavioral psychologists, is the substitution of anthropomorphic subjectivism for scientific theoretical constructs. If all explanations from human purposes or intentions were thus excluded, then the behavioral sciences would develop as did the physical sciences in the age of Copernicus, Kepler, and Galileo.

The philosophical theorists of action argue, on the contrary, that it is impossible to reduce or to translate into the language of physical science all concepts requisite to explain human behavior:

> To explain a piece of behavior . . . is to give a reason for it, to mention its aim or purpose, or to point to the rules that govern it. . . . Since behavior is essentially normative, . . . it is logically impossible to explain how men behave if we restrict ourselves to the purely descriptive language available to physical science. There is no way of deducing from a knowledge of physiology, however thorough, that there is a rule in our society to the effect that an extended hand means 'I am about to turn to the right.' . . . [15]

In his book, Taylor concluded, after careful analysis, that it is impossible, on logical grounds alone, to decide in favor of either teleological or mechanistic explanations. Thus he did not claim to demonstrate that it is impossible in principle to provide adequate mechanistic explanations of human behavior in a social context. Yet he found those explanations used by behavioral psychologists to be confused and unfruitful. His analysis left reductionists in a difficult position. In order to establish mechanical causal laws of human behavior, they must demonstrate that it is possible to describe all events in such a way that they are not linked logically or conceptually to any other events.

In a later paper, "Neutrality in Political Science," Taylor's target was the behavioral movement in American political science after World War II.[16] Central to it was the distinction behavioralists made between the scientific description of empirical facts and the normative evaluation of different courses of action. Behavioralists claimed that by divorcing themselves from political philosophy, they had made their subject into a dispassionate study of the facts without philosophical presuppositions and value biases. In time, the more cautious among them came to doubt the possibility of setting aside values altogether. Yet they held that as social science becomes more mature, it will be increasingly able to purge itself of value judgments.

In any case, they asserted, the logical distinction between facts and values remains. Scientific findings are neutral. It is always illegitimate to move from facts to values, from political science to political philosophy. If applied to policies, the scientific findings of political science can tell us how to realize our values or goals. But these can at best be clarified, but never scientifically justified. Before any set of facts, we may adopt any number of value positions.

Taylor, for his part, asserted that "facts" always must be interpreted from a given framework of explanation that supports an associated value position. This framework contains its own norms for assessing polities and policies. Thus behavioral scientists are in the same position as political philosophers. All need theoretical frameworks to delimit their areas of inquiry. Theoretical discovery is the delineation of the important dimensions for the range of phenomena concerned. Taylor's position is not purely negative—that theory is impossible because there is no way of attaining neutrality. Rather he asserts that Plato, Aristotle, Hobbes, Hegel, and Marx all delineated crucial dimensions of variation. For them, explaining and judging were inseparable. Their language and conceptual framework enabled them to do both.

Taylor then turned to the work of Lipset, Almond, and Lasswell. He contends that those dimensions of variation specified by their ostensibly neutral, empirical theories have two functions. They negate dimensions crucial to other theories they regard as normative; they support a theory of their own. When he sets out a theoretical framework, a theorist cannot fail to include some conception of human needs, wants, and purposes.

> In general we can see this arising in the following way: the framework gives us as it were the geography of the range of phenomena in question, it tells us how they can vary, what are the major dimensions of variation. But since we are dealing with matters of great importance to human beings, a given map will have its own built-in value-slope. That is to say, a given dimension of variation will usually determine for itself how we are to judge of good or bad, because of its relation to obvious human wants and needs.[17]

To adopt a given framework is to restrict the range of value positions that may be defensibly adopted. Within that framework, certain arrangements or outcomes can be established as good without further argument. Rival conceptions of good cannot be adopted without producing decisively overriding considerations. Hence the framework is not neutral.

Even in delivering this attack, Taylor did not range himself with other philosophers, such as Peter Winch or A. R. Louch, who attempted to make a decisive "knockout" argument against the possibility of a causal social science.[18] But in his subsequent "Interpretation and the Sciences of Man," Taylor introduced notions taken from phenomenology and hermeneutics.[19] These types of philosophy are concerned with problems of meaning, especially those that grow out of interpreting texts.[20] Taylor here added them to his analysis of social science. He saw important consequences that followed from adopting one or another theory of meaning. The behavioralists are committed to an instrumentalist conception of politics because they hold a philosophical position that precludes the possibility of any communal decision or deliberation.

Man is a self-defining animal. With changes in his definition of himself come changes in what man is. As Wittgenstein argued, language is embedded in rules deriving from social practices. Thus, the range of meanings open to members of two different societies is very different. Such variations in meaning have no interest for behavioral political science, which identifies them as purely subjective. Taylor argues that such meanings are intersubjective, and are of great importance to anyone explaining social action.

To the extent that behavioral political scientists notice intersubjective meanings, they attempt to deal with them by the reduction to "consensus." But this practice is unsatisfactory. The term "consensus" refers to beliefs and values that could be the property of one, many, or all persons in a society. But intersubjective meanings could not be the property of a single person because they have their root in social practices that cannot be conceived as a set of individual actions. They are modes of social relations, of mutual action.

The example Taylor uses to make this point and establish its significance is his contrast between negotiations in our society and those in a traditional Japanese village. Our notion of negotiation is contractual, bound up with the sharply distinguished identities of individual parties who may accept or reject offers. Traditional Japanese villages, on the other hand, relied on unanimous decisions as the basis of social life. They could not function in the event that groups formed around distinct interests.

Thus our conception of negotiation as bargaining among autonomous parties and groups could have no meaning. What is involved here is not just a different vocabulary, but a different social reality. Yet the language in part constitutes the reality. Neither can be reduced to the other. Although those negotiating may vary in individual beliefs and attitudes, what they do not bring into the negotiations is the set of ideas and norms which constitutes negotiating itself.

Taylor concludes that behavioral political science cannot treat either common or intersubjective meanings; therefore it denies the possibility of any communal decision or deliberation. This categorical denial of meaning to a subject that is a "we" rather than an "I" derives from the epistemology of logical empiricism. Because of such methodological individualism, politics must be viewed as purely instrumental. Such a view establishes the primacy of the private over the public sphere. The instrumental view of politics leaves no room for the political conceived as the collective decision of the community through deliberation and based on a determination of the common good.

All these points are clearly argued in Taylor's contribution to this book. But a point made elsewhere needs to be stated in order to see one potential consequence of the argument. This point involves the introduction of interpretation into the study of man.

The logical empiricist opposes any conduct of inquiry based on interpretation on the grounds that it would violate the requirements of intersubjective verification. Science must be based upon "brute data," the validity of which cannot be questioned by offering another interpretation or reading. But if, as Taylor proposes, the subject of social science becomes not brute data, but only the readings of meanings, how are we to decide among conflicting meanings? Without the verification model of the logical empiricists, there would be no way of resolving what is called the hermeneutical circle. What happens if you don't understand after I explain why my interpretation makes sense of something that didn't appear to have any meaning or previously seemed contradictory? To this question, Taylor gave an answer in his earlier treatment of interpretation. It comes to the assertion that we must choose among our divergent options in politics and in life. "A study of the science of man is inseparable from an examination of the options among which men must choose."[21]

In a brief paper, Taylor has gone far toward providing an alternative to the behavioral philosophy of science. Yet some nagging questions remain. It will be interesting to see whether Taylor will address himself to the question of what a political science based on his proposed alternative might look like. In his book on Hegel, he uses his exposition and critique of that philosopher as a vehicle for expressing his own ideas. To some extent he indicates what he takes to be the most promising lines of development for political philosophy. His discussion of "expressivism" is stimulating, although it cannot be taken up here. He provides an assessment of what is to be learned from Hegel and Marx, and of where they went wrong. But what has not as yet emerged is a clear exposition of a political science based upon his countermodel to that of logical empiricism. Until that is provided, the standard version may be expected to remain in place.[22]

Mihailo Marković's paper stands in a complex relationship to the others in this volume. He is a member of the Yugoslavian group known as *Praxis* Marxists. In his own work, he has sought to combine Marxist humanism with the analytical training he received from A. J. Ayer. As will appear, he has been sensitive to other influences as well. Although his use of critical theory resembles that made by Sheldon Wolin in his paper, Marković is perhaps closer to Charles Taylor than to any other contributor. Both value highly the critical, as well as the humanist, aspects of Marx's thought; both regard Marx's treatment of politics not only as incomplete, but as requiring substantial amendment.

The central point of Marković's argument is his assertion that although Marx never systematically developed a political philosophy, "the implicit deep structure of 'the critique of political economy'" developed by Marx remains the best "foundation of a radical, critical, humanist-oriented thinking." To each of these terms, Marković attaches a distinctive meaning.

By his use of "radical," Marković refers to one of Marx's characteristic moves in his analysis of economy and society: the assertion that beneath surface appearances is to be found a complex of deeper underlying causes. To this statement Marković adds an existentialist dimension by his view that irreducible moral choices are forced upon anyone who takes seriously the material social conditions under which humans live. His phrase for a political philosophy so focused is "the critique of the human condition." Here the concept of a "human condition" derives from existentialism; that of "critique" from Marxism in general, and from the Frankfurt School in particular.

When he applies his method to late capitalist societies, Marković does so as a Marxist who regards them as fundamentally flawed. He does not rule out the possibility of significant change produced either by violent or non-violent means. The choice of a course of action ought to be determined, he believes, on the basis of a pragmatic and empirical judgment.

Marković also applies his critique to governments that regard themselves as Marxist and socialist. It is one thing for a political philosopher living in such a society to maintain that labor under capitalism leads to alienation; it is something else to assert that under socialism the same effect can be produced by one-party rule and a bureaucratic monopoly in decision-making. For this kind of unrelenting critique, Marković and seven other colleagues have been suspended from their teaching positions since 1975. Their journal, *Praxis*, can no longer be published in their own country.

What is the connection between Marković's application of "critique" and his emphasis upon the humanism of Marx? One clue is to be found in Marković's use of the concept of alienation to specify its antonyms: the self-realization of individuals, emancipation, and *praxis*. To ask what are the conditions of their attainment is to raise at the same time the question of how politics may either cause or combat alienation. Here Marković breaks with Marx when he asserts the value both of politics and political philosophy. Yet Marković's sketch of what a Marxist political philosophy might look like is itself grounded on what he describes as Marx's implicit program for deriving *praxis* from critique.

Marx's analysis of capitalism in his early writings derived from a theory of man and from a philosophical method that he failed to develop adequately. It is on the basis of this assessment that Marković, like many other socialists, has sought to make explicit Marx's philosophical anthropology and method. By close study and criticism of capitalist economic and social relations, Marx made it possible to specify the altogether antithetical principles that could be realized in such a society once it had been emancipated from the repressive and exploitative domination of its ruling class. Yet Marx never went on to formulate these principles. This Marković attributes to Marx's hostile judgment of moral and political philosophy, which he thought to be necessarily nothing more than the statement of a purely abstract set of principles deriving from subjective intentions. In part Marković disagrees with this categorical dismissal, which, in his view, is connected to certain undesirable and unnecessary aspects of socialism in some countries. At the same time Marković reaffirms Marx's judgment that any political theory is acceptable to socialists only to the extent that it can produce effective action to transform the existing system of capitalistic economic relations.

Thus no notion is more significant to Marković than that of *praxis*.[23] Although the contrast between theory and practice has long been familiar to philosophers writing in English, Marković means something other than what that distinction usually implies. One helpful exposition of that difference distinguishes "high" uses of *praxis* from "low" senses of practice in English.[24]

Praxis was used by Aristotle to mark off the good life open only to free men in politics and morality. Aristotle distinguishes that term both from the activity necessary to maintain existence and from the work done by artisans. *Praxis* is thus the arena of the good life, and the sort of knowledge requisite to doing good is practical reason. Another contrast Aristotle makes is between *praxis* and *theoria*. *Theoria* is on a higher plane because when a wise person exercises *theoria* through reason, what is contemplated is unchanging being. Yet both *theoria* and *praxis* are acceptable ways of life open to the free man. Hannah Arendt developed an analogous distinction between the public sphere of shared words and deeds where humans realize their humanity through action and the private sphere of the household or workplace. Although she makes a place for what she calls work, she finds mere labor incompatible with citizenship.

The incomparably best theory of *praxis* Marković finds in Marx, who took a very different view of labor. Marx treated labor as the distinctive activity that transforms the materials of labor into those products needed by human beings. Thus labor shapes decisively the structure within which we live. By and through it, the activities of producers assume material form, thus realizing potentialities and, to varying degrees, fulfilling material needs.

Thus regarded, *praxis* is a generic human activity. It may lead either to alienating, or to truly human, activity. Productive labor forms one part of *praxis*; its other components are critique and revolutionary activity. In Marković's restatement, the concept includes both self-realization and self-determination within the context of human sociability, cooperation, and rationality. *Praxis* is both positive and normative; as such, it is the antithesis of alienation.

Despite his identification with this central strand of Marx's thought, Marković accepts some criticisms that have been made of Marxism as a political philosophy. Marx all too easily dismissed as superficial all previous theories of politics. This dismissal led to Marx's failure, and that of those who took him as their guide, to acknowledge as a problem for socialism the organization of power, whether it be of the party or of the state. Thus Marković joins a growing number of Marxists who address the distinctive organization of power under socialism. Socialist concepts of power create the possibility of abuses by the single legal party. Marković asserts that bureaucracy and centralization, if unchecked, may endanger the good life socialism was meant to create. Socialism is not by its nature in any sense incapable of dealing with these abuses, but they must be identified and means must be found for limiting power that is at present unrestrained.

Many other Marxists who have made similar criticisms have stopped short of the project Marković undertakes in the last section of his paper. That is nothing less than the charting of the elements requisite to an adequate Marxist political philosophy. Marković confronts these issues because he accepts some of the philosophical premises held by other contributors to this volume. He denies that political philosophy expresses purely personal preferences, or that it is normative only, and thus incapable of that objective knowledge attainable only by science. Rather he stresses not just the possibility, but the necessity, of getting on with the task of formulating a Marxist political philosophy that combines critique with *praxis*. This philosophy will not be positivist; it will combine both evaluation and description, and it will take into account the necessity for socialism to develop its own way of responding adequately to the distinctive problems of political philosophy.

Not the least of these problems for socialism, as for other forms, is that of rights: both the rights of individuals and of minorities. Nor have participation and self-government by citizens become a reality under socialist governments any more than they have under capitalist democracies. Although Marković does not deal with the question of political commentators, presumably he would share Wolin's concern that they be permitted to engage in criticism of a sort that allows alternatives to be conceived and discussed. In short, by his proposals Marković has placed on the agenda of socialists almost all those issues raised by his colleagues in the field of political philosophy.[25]

Allan Bloom and J.G.A. Pocock, however, were invited to deal with a somewhat different set of issues. Their concerns involve teaching past political philosophers through the close study of texts, on the one side; and, on the other, stating a new and alternative conception of what it means to study political theory historically. The two papers come together at some points, such as the question of which books ought to be read, and the relationship among their authors. The issue of what is meant by a tradition, considered in terms of political philosophy, receives attention in both papers. But the foci of interest, the theoretical frameworks, and the conceptions of political theory are otherwise divergent.

In his paper, Bloom makes an eloquent appeal for the study of political philosophy through texts alone. Political philosophy he describes as "the quest for knowledge of the best way of life, of the most comprehensive good or of justice and the best regime." Such a study depends, as he sees it, upon the existence of a knowable good. But this is denied by the most powerful intellectual forces of our time: positivism, historicism, and cultural relativism.

The value of teaching political philosophy through texts is that it enables the teacher to purge his students of received opinions that stand in the way of his thinking philosophically about politics. These obstacles include all categories of thought and speech derived from contemporary or recent philosophy. Thus, by the closest possible teaching of the texts, and of these only, can the teacher of political philosophy bring his student back to the pre-scientific or pre-philosophical natural world.

For the choice of texts, Bloom suggests two criteria: general agreement about who were the great political philosophers, and inferences from what the great thinkers say about each other. From this consensus emerges a small list of philosophers worth study, and a range of positions that warrant consideration. Bloom believes that future professors of political philosophy ought to be trained to preserve this tradition. Although arguments from authority have no place in philosophical discourse, it is nevertheless the case that respect for tradition may keep alive what otherwise would not be taken seriously. As to the question of what constitutes a tradition, Bloom and Pocock do not agree.

Bloom argues that there are no universally applicable rules of interpretation: Every author must be understood from within. Openness can be taught by making students see the world through the lenses of a great political philosopher. Not many books can be so read, but to study a work of genuine worth in this way is to learn how to read any book. The chief rule is that everything in the text must be taken seriously. No argument is to be dismissed on the basis of historical scholarship, or the judgment of what the philosopher must have meant, made from the vantage point of our superior knowledge about him, his age, and his presuppositions.

Much of what Bloom has written could be accepted, *mutatis mutandis*, by almost all the contributors to this book. His ardor is contagious. He catches the excitement of political philosophy when it is first encountered through the books of the great political philosophers. He stresses the importance of learning to understand their questions as they understood them, and of confronting the original arguments with all their lasting power and capacity to illuminate.

Those who have taught political philosophy will also recognize the characteristic obstacles to learning Bloom describes. Students everywhere seem to read little, and to lack training in coping with sustained abstract reasoning. Few know the Bible or the imaginative work of the past. History means not much to them. There is a general reluctance to learn and work in any language other than their own.

Bloom's emphasis upon the importance of using great texts in teaching political philosophy is thus in part pedagogical, based on an assessment of what are the actual obstacles and resistances. His contention is based on long experience, and

confirmed by the staying power over the centuries of the authors and the works to which he refers. A curriculum such as
"Greats" at Oxford was and still is based on detailed analysis
of such books. However, Bloom's method, formulated in its
strongest form, comes to more than this, for he would
exclude in the study of texts all categories of thought derived
from recent or contemporary philosophy except in studying
that recent or contemporary philosophy. This method puts
him in sharp opposition not only to Pocock, but to everyone
else writing in this volume. The vehemence of this judgment
may startle some readers who wish further argument and
analysis. These may be most concisely drawn from a remark-
able essay describing the position of modern political thought
written by Bloom's teacher, the late Professor Leo Strauss.[26]

Professor Strauss's work first came to the attention of
English-speaking political philosophers during the 1930s,
when he left Nazi Germany. Once established in the United
States, he found philosophy and politics under the influence of
philosophical tendencies he knew and held responsible for
much of what had gone wrong in Germany. After World War
II, Professor Strauss was among the first to attack positivism
and historicism, not only in political philosophy, but in the
study of politics. At the time when Max Weber's work and
method were being uncritically accepted and imitated, Professor Strauss launched a powerful attack upon them. He called
into question Weber's advocacy of value-free analysis, his
theory that all values are purely emotive, and the concomitant
distinction between normative and empirical statements. Of
course Weber was neither the first nor the worst of the political thinkers who had been deeply impressed by positivism
and historicism. These powerful currents of modern thought
had replaced all teachings of natural right, classical or modern,
and denied the possibility of political philosophy.

To his adverse judgment on Weber, Professor Strauss
added an indictment of behavioralist political science. His
counter-arguments were: 1) it is impossible to study social
phenomena without making value judgments; 2) the rejection

of the validity of value judgments is based on the assumption that conflicts among conflicting value systems cannot be rationally resolved, an assumption for which no proof has yet been demonstrated; 3) the belief that scientific knowledge, i.e., that of modern science, is the highest attainable implies a depreciation of pre-scientific knowledge. But this remains the prerequisite to the type of reflection that leads to practical action by the citizen; 4) because of its emphasis on observed facts, positivism produces a distorted political science which makes the modern western world into the model for all human societies.

Positivism itself falls prey to the relativism produced by historicist thinking. Even modern science, in the light of historicism, came to be viewed as but one form of human understanding that is itself not superior to alternative forms. Professor Strauss's characterization of how the most developed form of historicism differs from positivism is crucial to understanding Bloom's view of the present position of political philosophy:

> 1) It [historicism] abandons the distinction between facts and values; every understanding, however theoretical, implies specific valuations. 2) It denies the authoritative character of modern science, which appears as only one form among many of man's thinking orientations in the world. 3) It refuses to regard the historical process as fundamentally progressive, or . . . reasonable. . . . Historicism rejects the question of the good society, that is to say, of *the* good society. The crucial issue concerns the status of those permanent characteristics of humanity, such as the distinction between the noble and the base.[27]

Professor Strauss concluded by pondering the fact that the man whom he considered the greatest thinker of the twentieth century and its most radical historicist Heidegger, welcomed the advent of the German political decision of 1933 as a dispensation of fate.

Impressed by the crisis in politics and in thought about

politics, Strauss was persuaded that neither science nor history could serve the function performed in the past by political philosophy. He was also persuaded that because all modern thought derived either from the scientific project or from historicism, it was incapable of raising in any serious way the question of the good society. Strauss's life work was an attempt to see whether the refutations of the old philosophers by the new were adequate. It was in this way that he tried to reopen questions that were considered closed. He argued that in order to question the premises of our thought we need to begin by doubting them radically and by trying to see them as they would be seen by their opponents. As a result, almost all of Strauss's writings take the form of close studies of the texts of writers, ancient and modern. These studies seek to avoid using as interpretive principles those premises he was investigating, except when their use was native to the text. He thus tried to revive the quarrel between the ancients and the moderns.

Strauss's analysis of modern thought certainly is striking. Yet many contributors to this volume reject the fact-value distinction and other characteristics of positivism, which they agree makes political philosophy impossible. What implications does their rejection have for Bloom's insistence that modern philosophy cannot generate a political philosophy? Perhaps an explicit statement of his reasons for this insistence would make his case more plausible. Until such a statement appears, those who do not accept his method in its entirety may find it difficult to accept any part of it. This would be regrettable, if it were to mean that teaching from texts could not be justified on other grounds. But surely there is a case for teaching at least undergraduates how to read a great book. Bernard Williams, in his essay, seems willing to concur that this is the way to begin philosophical instruction, although he might be more reluctant to agree that it is all that can or ought to be done.

J.G.A. Pocock's paper has both a positive and a negative program. He wishes to reject the notion that there is a unified and narratable history of political philosophy. This exclusion would apply to any scheme, including that division between ancients and moderns advocated by Bloom. Nor does Pocock agree that there are perennial positions that represent options, or that it is possible to study the history of political philosophy as that of a dialogue between the greats, no matter how far separated in time. And he denies that it makes historical sense to concentrate upon a canon of classics.

Pocock's objections derive from his belief that any canon generates unhistorical interpretation. This may happen in two ways. Imagined relationships between the authors figuring in the canon may distort their actual interests, and the later interpreter may apply a statement found in the canon to a situation inconceivable to its author. In an earlier collection of essays, Pocock saw the danger of such ways of treating political thought as particularly menacing to the historian who could not relate such imaginary constructs to the other materials he had to handle. Thus historians tended to avoid political ideas. Or else they retreated to procedures that reduced ideas to the byproducts of some more substantial and basic order of things. Historians lacked an autonomous method that would enable them to treat political ideas as historical phenomena, even as historical events—as things happening in a context which defines the kind of events they were.

These issues figure in the title of the paper presented here, as well as in Pocock's recent book, *The Machiavellian Moment: Florentine Political Thought and the Atlantic Republican Tradition*.[28] His positive program is to show, not that the ideas of political philosophers make history in some idealist sense, but rather that:

> Men think by communicating language systems; these systems help constitute both their conceptual worlds and their authority structures, or social worlds related to these; the conceptual and social worlds may each be seen as a context to the other. . . . The individual's thinking may now be viewed as a social event, an act of

communication and response, . . . and as a historical event, a moment in a process of transformation of the system. . . .[29]

Thus he is proposing, not that we should study the history of political philosophy, but rather that we should study political philosophy historically. So considered, political philosophy turns out to be pluralistic. As he argues in his paper, political society is so constructed that its communication networks can never be entirely closed. Language from one level may be heard and responded to at another; paradigms may migrate from one context to another. Similarly, ideas may be controlled by later understandings, which cannot be exclusively controlled by anyone in the communication network, including the thinker who first formulated the concept. These consequences are significant for both the philosopher and the historian. Their political implications lie in the liberal and pluralistic rendition of the concept of tradition that distinguished it from more conservative treatments.

In *The Machiavellian Moment*, Pocock treats both Florentine political thinkers in the fifteenth century and those later theorists in England and America who took them as guides to republicanism. In Pocock's scheme, these thinkers are interpreted as acting within conceptual and social limits. At the same time, they help transform the system of political languages and the social world within which authority is communicated and distributed by linguistic means.

His book begins with the problems that arose for those in Florentine history who sought to revive the ideal of active participation in citizenship. This Aristotelian theory had to be applied in a very different context. How was the political nature of man, as described by Aristotle, to be fulfilled within the changed temporal framework and values of a Christian viewpoint that denied the possibility of any secular fulfillment on earth? The European mind could then conceive of three answers only: custom, grace, and fortune.

By the Machiavellian moment, Pocock means two things:

1) the importance of temporal categories, as they existed for medieval and early modern Europeans; 2) the specific moment when the Florentine Republic had to confront its own situation. How could it attain stability in the midst of irrational events? In this conceptual vocabulary, the virtue of the citizen was threatened both by fortune and corruption. Machiavelli was one among other thinkers concerned to explore common problems arising out of this conceptual language. Nor did the story end with them. The Machiavellian moment had a real and continuing history; its legacy was the "concepts of balanced government, dynamic *virtu*, and the role of arms and property in shaping the civic personality." In the second part of his book, Pocock carries his story into British and American thought in the seventeenth and eighteenth centuries, showing how republican and Machiavellian concepts become imbedded in this tradition. The crucial role was played by James Harrington, the complete edition of whose works Pocock has just given us.[30]

In *The Machiavellian Moment*, Pocock identifies and traces the origin and mutations of a political tradition of discourse which had an important effect upon Anglo-American and European perceptions of politics, society, and history. These perceptions led to action of a sort that would not have been possible without these categories. By telling how and why this tradition came into being, Pocock puts Machiavelli and Harrington into a new position. He also causes us to view Locke and Burke from a perspective sharply altered by his treatment. Thus British and American political thought take on meanings they did not previously have.

Although he sees some potential dangers, Pocock is not troubled by the accusation that his method is historicist in the sense condemned by Bloom. Pocock holds that political philosophers ought to be trained to consider historically what has been written by their predecessors, that is to take seriously the actual categories and options available to them. The philosopher will be better prepared to receive and comprehend information of diverse provenience and meaning. Such training will enhance his capacity to view himself as a historical being, and he will come to understand that though this message is itself conditioned, it can nevertheless modify the structures that condition it. Not all the consequences of his acts of thought will be those he foresees or intends. He shares the world with those using other methods which may limit or enrich his own.

Pocock's essay is cast in the form of a dialogue between himself and a philosopher, presumably one working in the analytical style. When Pocock discusses the history of political philosophy, he seems to expect more criticism from philosophers than is actually made in Williams's discussion of the subject. As long as the historical study of political ideas is carried on in terms of the changing sets of concepts societies use to characterize and legitimize their organization, there is no reason for philosophers to object. Nothing in Pocock's method, either programmatically or in actual use, suggests that he is proposing it as a substitute for what political philosophers are now doing. Actually, his interest in language and its relationship to thought derives in part from the concerns of analytical philosophy. Those who write in his style, like Quentin Skinner, are increasingly concerned with working out the implications of the theory of action for the historical study of political philosophy. Analytical philosophers are more likely to feel flattered than menaced by such attention.

The historical study of political philosophy, then, can be carried out to the satisfaction and profit of historians and philosophers. Nor is it difficult to see how it could become of interest to sociologists, especially those working in *Wissenssoziologie*. Yet it may be asked whether the charge of historicism raised by Bloom has altogether been answered. In what sense is the study of history qualitatively different from the study of philosophy? This problem arises for those teaching students who may never again take a course in political philosophy. The question then becomes: How ought students be trained when they first encounter political philosophy?

It is at this point that the papers of Walzer and Wolin

both raise issues that connect to the concerns of Pocock and Bloom. Essentially, each of these papers on political education presupposes a training applicable to practical political action. Presumably that training is what teachers should emphasize when teaching students studying political philosophy for the first time. Yet much depends upon how a particular type of teaching is done. The Oxford tradition of tutorial teaching was also developed as a way of getting undergraduates to divest themselves of preconceptions and to teach them how to confront an old and still formidable text. Yet some of those who have passed through this process have observed that students may be given cues as to whether they are meant to be reverential or critical, academically precise or simply echoes of their teacher's views. Do all teachers who use texts do so without indicating how they ought to be interpreted? Do not significant silences, implicit or explicit approval or disapproval on the teacher's part, also create a set of intimations not lost upon students?

Thus it may be good for all those who teach political philosophy and its history to consider what ought to be taught undergraduates and advanced students: No doubt their conclusions will be not unaffected by their responses to the positions argued by Bloom and Pocock.

The papers by Ronald Dworkin, Michael Walzer, and Sheldon Wolin explore the relationship between political philosophy and political education. Dworkin considers the potential contributions of political philosophy to our thinking about the nature of law, rights, and the legal system. Indeed, he argues that the central issues of jurisprudence are, at their core, issues of moral and political philosophy. Walzer argues for developing a type of political philosophy that applies general principles to those moral and political issues faced not only by official decision-makers, but by all citizens. Wolin takes up the important connections between political theory and political commentary.

There is an interesting relationship between the papers of Dworkin and Walzer. Walzer finds much to admire in the training lawyers acquire in law schools, particularly that in the type of analysis and decision procedures used in hard cases. He argues that analogous training could provide a model for political education. Dworkin, however, is less pleased with law schools, whose training he regards as excessively positivist, and ultimately trivial. His theory of jurisprudence is that landmark cases ought to be decided on the basis of principle, not policy. The task of providing adequate principles must be the work of political philosophers. Yet, he argues, law schools have not yet made adequate provision for philosophers to participate in legal education.

Although their treatments of these shared concerns differ, Walzer and Dworkin both conceive of theory as prescribing courses of action; they reject all notions of it as neutral, descriptive, and uncontestable. Thus, explicitly or implicitly, they reject positivism in jurisprudence, behavioralism in the social sciences, realism, utilitarianism, and moral relativism. Wolin, although making adverse judgments of these positions, does so from his own theory of politics as vision, and from his adaptation of critical theory. As a result, although both he and Walzer directly address the problems of applying political theory to the public realm, they do so from different positions and with different purposes in mind. Neither shares all of Dworkin's concerns and priorities. In their disagreements, as much in their shared conviction that political philosophy ought to contribute to the public realm, these three essays may be regarded as a dialogue on how best to conduct political education.

Walzer's instrument of analysis is moral philosophy in the analytical mode. Its focus is the agent who must act on the basis of what he knows, and whose decision must take into account the often conflicting principles he holds. This model Walzer applies to political decision-making in democratic societies. In this view, not only public officials, but also many ordinary citizens anticipate, review, and replay political decisions. Political education ought to prepare both citizens and leaders for making moral decisions. To clarify his own model, he contrasts it to another he calls "realist." This model is similar to what Taylor has designated as the instrumental view of politics. For the realist, Walzer argues, decision-making comes down to maximizing values beyond rational dispute such as that of national security.

To perform the tasks of public office so defined, a special type of character is implicitly recommended. The ideal decision-maker is, for the realist, unwavering, hard-headed, cool, calculating, ruthless, ready (in Herman Kahn's phrase) "to think the unthinkable." Moral concerns and considerations need not concern such a person. Indeed, to do so is to inject private for public rules of action.

To Walzer, as to Williams, this realist model of decision-making is in fact a moral position, and any claim it might have to our attention is the result of moral claims and prescriptions. Thus it is argued that national security decisions made on the basis of morality will lead to the loss of lives without any commensurate return. Walzer makes his points against realism in the first chapter of his recent book, *Just and Unjust Wars*.[31] Again, like Williams, Walzer rejects the realists' notion of rationality, which they define as making the best possible decision, no matter what the alternatives. Walzer argues that rationality must include an assessment of the situation. It may be that rational moral agents ought to refuse to accept responsibility for impossible situations not created by moral agency. Finally, both Walzer and Williams argue that the arithmetic used by realists is also faulty. Here they contend that recent work in welfare economics and decision theory casts doubt about the model of realist calculation.

Yet the realist model has been legitimized and institutionalized by universities in their teaching of politics. The moralist model is regarded as suspect. Despite the fact that political leaders and citizens consider themselves to be moral, and not infrequently make decisions on the basis of moral considerations, the teaching of politics excludes them. This situation Walzer challenges in both his paper and his book.

To the realist procedure, he contrasts his own, which takes

seriously the moral principles of leaders and citizens. He deliberately chooses hard cases, in which those deciding must use conflicting sets of principles, such as national security and individual rights.

In Walzer's view, what is most needed are disciplined procedures for applying general moral principles to particular cases. The absence of such procedures has led critics of what Walzer calls the "moralist model" to assert that general principles of morality offer no guidance whatever to decisionmakers who have to decide what to do in concrete situations. Such an assertion overlooks the fact that this is not what general principles are meant to do. Walzer's proposal is designed to create a new subject in political philosophy to perform the functions of what was known as casuistry before Pascal gave the term a pejorative connotation in his polemics against the Jesuits. The technical meaning is still preserved in the *Oxford English Dictionary*, where casuistry is defined as "that part of ethics which resolves cases of conscience, applying the general rules of . . . morality to particular instances which disclose special circumstances or conflicting duties."

The most promising method for developing and teaching such a subject Walzer finds in the case method used in law schools to train future lawyers and judges. In the common law, judges make decisions; these are both anticipated and second-guessed by other lawyers. In law schools, students must, as part of their training, learn to reach decisions by going through the same process used by judges to weigh, reason, and construct arguments in hard cases already decided or in hypothetical arguments.

Such a training for the political education of citizens would have two objectives: to school citizens how to make moral decisions as future actors in politics or as vicarious decisionmakers; to generate in the community at large a tradition of discourse with a shared knowledge of how such cases have been decided in the past. Although political leaders still would have responsibility for the moral decisions they must make, they would do so, like judges, in the context of precedent, argument, anticipation, and criticism. As one part of political science, such training would combine political theory with a particular kind of history.

Not much work of this sort is being done. Moral philosophers either operate on the level of metatheory, a level of generality that passes over the problems of actual moral decisions in politics; or tend to take their examples from non-political life. In the past, historians usually have not performed such analyses. Given the present direction of historical inquiry, they seem more likely to imitate the positivism of the social sciences than to attempt what is here proposed.

Several objections to Walzer's proposals present themselves, and Walzer anticipates them as he develops his argument. He assumes that there is a moral law with general principles that are acknowledged even when human beings cannot or will not live up to them. Thus it is possible to discuss practical morality without referring to the foundations of ethics. But he does not suggest

> . . . that we can do nothing more than describe the judgments and justifications that people commonly put forward. We can analyze these moral claims, seek out their coherence, lay bare the principles that they exemplify. We can reveal commitments that go deeper than partisan allegiance and the urgencies of battle. . . . And then we can expose the hypocrisy of soldiers and statesmen. . . . We are rarely called upon to invent new ethical principles. If we did that, our criticism would not be comprehensible to the people whose behavior we wanted to condemn. Rather we hold such people to their own principles.[32]

Walzer shares with other contributors to this volume the disposition to deny that ethical relativism is a tenable position, that moral judgments are simply subjective judgments that vary with interest and situation. Like Charles Taylor, and for the same reasons, Walzer denies the fact-value distinctions held by many social scientists. He stresses the significance of the fact that we use a specifically evaluative language over and beyond that used to express feelings, liking, choice, and to give orders. Yet it is possible to make this point and still to conclude that an appeal to a vocabulary of shared evaluation may not necessarily succeed. It may be that the forms of moral life in our own society are not integrated. Alasdair MacIntyre argues, for example, that in our society we live with an inheritance of moral vocabularies from not just one, but a number of moralities. Each has its proposed end or ends, its set of rules, list of virtues, but they do not coincide. "Between the adherents of rival moralities and between the adherent of one morality and the adherents of none, there exists no court of appeal, no impersonal moral standard."[33] Controversies about the nature of ethics express the fundamental moral cleavages of society.

In *Just and Unjust Wars*, Walzer tacitly replies to this argument in his statement of the purpose and method that underlie his choice of the moral theory of war as a test case.

> I want to account for the ways in which men and women who are not lawyers but simply citizens (and sometimes soldiers) argue about war and to expound the terms we commonly use. I am concerned precisely with the present structure of the moral world. My starting point is the fact that we do argue, often to different purposes, to be sure, but in a mutually comprehensible fashion; else there would be no point in *arguing*. We justify our conduct; we judge the conduct of others.[34]

Walzer does not stress the elements of agreement in the moral theory of war, but rather the tensions within the theory that make it problematic. These tensions make choice difficult and painful.

> The tensions are summed up in the dilemma of winning and fighting well. This the military form of the ends/ means problem, the central issue in political ethics. . . . The resolution, if it works, must be relevant to the

choices faced in politics generally. For war is the hardest place; if comprehensive and consistent moral judgments are possible there, they are possible everywhere.[35]

Another criticism of Walzer's assumptions is to be found in the position taken by Sheldon Wolin. In his view, the political theorist should not accept the framework within which political actors must make their decisions. Rather the theorist ought to gain sufficent distance so as to acquire a more adequate perspective on political things. The essential element is criticism of ordinary moral judgments and political perspectives. Positive action, to be worth anything, must be based on theory that, rather than accepting existing interpretations, has called them into question.

Walzer's reply stated his view that political education is best performed, not by contrasting different forms of grand theory, but by applying one form to specific cases. In his paper, he contends that it is not only in schools but also in politics that we acquire our political education. This applies to ethical problems as well.

Even in a form of politics as little given to discussion of fundamental human rights and values as Marxism, the analysis of a particular case generated both realist and moralist positions. Walzer is referring to the Bolshevik suppression of rebels in Kronstadt in 1921. Until the beginning of World War II, radicals worked out their own ethical positions by deciding what they would have done about the Kronstadt rebels.

As for the proper definition of political theory, Walzer remarks that it can be put to different uses. No doubt it can be described in grander terms than those he proposes in this paper. Nevertheless, political education has particular significance in a democracy. Those who teach politics ought to attend to the genuinely moral concerns of those who make real or vicarious decisions in hard cases.

It has already been remarked that Walzer and Dworkin share an interest in what happens when a hard case is decided by judges. Dworkin, in his paper and even more in *Taking Rights Seriously*, stresses that significant cases are decided by judges who must make use of contested interpretation.[36] Thus he is making an argument in jurisprudence that is important in moral and political philosophy as well. Indeed, Dworkin argues that in hard cases, judges must be understood as deriving their arguments from principles rather than from policy. These principles are best understood in terms of individual rights.

Dworkin's emphasis upon contestable or problematical propositions of law stands in sharp contrast to the interpretation given by legal positivists and by political scientists using sociological jurisprudence. Legal positivists define what law is by giving a non-problematical account of the necessary and sufficient conditions for it to be properly so-called. Political scientists, who study law according to behavioral canons, refuse to discuss hard cases in terms of judges following rules. Precisely because there is no agreement about what it means to follow a rule in such cases, practitioners of sociological jurisprudence assert that rules cannot be the subject of quantitative scientific inquiry. If every investigator were to use a different sense of the term "following rules", neither objective data nor cumulative progress would be possible. Thus those who study judicial behavior by behavioral methods perform a translation into terms and problems they can study meaningfully. They substitute for the study of rules, inquiry into the social background and prior allegiance of judges. On the basis of such data, they attempt to predict what position a judge will take in a hard case. If the background and allegiance of a judge determine his decision, then it may be inferred that he is not following rules.

Dworkin's position is that, although such information is interesting and useful for other purposes, it does not clarify the issues of principle. Lawyers know that judges often disagree and that their decisions are affected by their backgrounds. But does this mean that judges differ on the nature and point of fundamental legal principles or that there are no such principles? Should the disagreement among judges be regretted, accepted as inevitable, or applauded as dynamic? How do these positions connect to those issues of political obligation and law enforcement faced by lawyers and judges? By rephrasing questions involved in hard cases, political scientists have eliminated all significant questions of principle. Dworkin here rejects reductionism in jurisprudence, just as Taylor did in dealing with the philosophy of science.

Dworkin also attacks what he describes as the ruling theory of Anglo-American jurisprudence, a theory that combines legal positivism with economic utilitarianism. Any theory that defines law in terms of its non-problematical necessary and sufficient conditions is, in his view, positivistic. The best statement of this position, Dworkin believes, was made by H.L.A. Hart. Hart distinguishes two sorts of binding rules: those that are accepted because they are binding social rules, and those that are valid because of a secondary rule stipulating how legal rules are to be identified. Such a secondary rule consists of recognition by the citizens and officials of a community. The province of law is identified by recognition of its rules in the operation of the governmental apparatus of legislatures, courts, and police. To what extent the rules are recognized is demonstrated by the behavior of citizens and officials, by the ultimate arguments they accept as showing the validity of a rule. The central notion of legal positivism, according to Dworkin, is its formulation of a single non-problematical test for what constitutes law. This, in his view, makes it impossible to recognize those standards that are not rules.

Of these standards, the most important are principles and policies. In *Taking Rights Seriously*, Dworkin distinguishes these terms:

> I call a 'policy' that kind of standard that sets out a goal to be reached, generally an improvement in some economic, political, or social feature of the community (though some goals are negative . . .).
>
> I call a 'principle' a standard that is to be observed, not

because it will advance or secure an economic, political, or social situation deemed desirable, but because it is a requirement of justice or fairness or some other dimension of morality. Thus the standard that automobile accidents are to be decreased is a policy, and the standard that no man may profit by his own wrong a principle.[37]

Dworkin goes on to argue that any adequate analysis of legal obligation must find a place for the part played by principles in reaching landmark decisions of law (such as *Macpherson* v. *Buick*, which he discusses in his paper). But principles may be accounted for in two ways: first, by saying that some principles are binding as law, and therefore must be considered as such by judges and lawyers; second, by denying that principles may bind, as do some rules. Dworkin finds only the first account acceptable. Principles provide the best justification of settled rules of law, and are themselves true propositions of law. Ultimately these principles are derived from the rights of individuals: legal rights, even those not explicitly stated; and moral and political rights, even against the welfare of the majority.

This position, however, is not reached in Dworkin's contribution to this volume. Instead of considering it in the light of arguments found only in *Taking Rights Seriously*, it is more appropriate to state briefly Dworkin's argument against utilitarian justifications from policy. Dworkin rejects utilitarianism because, even in its most complex formulations, it may be used to deny the rights of citizens to be treated as equals. Here similar arguments made by Williams and Walzer against utilitarianism ought to be recalled.

In his paper, Dworkin demonstrates how, by making principles part of the law, his jurisprudence would greatly increase the contributions political philosophers could make to legal studies and judicial practice—contributions Dworkin believes are badly needed, particularly in judicial treatments of the equal rights amendment and legislation prohibiting classifications by race. To Dworkin, it seems more likely that political philosophers could supply the general theory of equality than that lawyers or judges could do so. Such a theory would have to provide an independently appealing concept of equality that could be inspected and justified as a statement of political morality. Only a problematical theory could do this, and thus break down the distinction between fact and value, between what is and what ought to be in law.

Sheldon Wolin, like Dworkin and Walzer, is concerned not with defending political theory, but with extending its role. This he wishes to do by making political commentary more theoretical. His first set of problems hinges on clarifying the concept of political commentary and determining its relationship to the activity of theorizing about politics.

Many major works by political theorists offer explicit judgments on the politics of their time. Some significant books were in fact originally written as pamphlets. Others, ostensibly more distant from contemporary events, justify or condemn theoretical positions of great importance to those undertaking political action. Thus, political theory is not a pure and objective branch of thought. Nor can it be without losing its interest, as Williams also remarks. Yet political theory and political commentary are different activities, as can be demonstrated by theorists who have also engaged in political commentary. Wolin's examples are Hegel, Marx, and Max Weber. In their newspaper articles and pamphlets, they pointedly address a diverse and unknown audience in language accessible to the layman. Nor do they require from their public knowledge and understanding of their general theory. Wolin, however, would not have a theorist engaged in commentary give up the distinctive perspective gained in the first instance by the effort to achieve distance from the immediacy of politics. "Rather he has used the theory to inform his commentary, and he has made of commentary an intimation of his theory."

The theorist who writes for a general public seeks to change the way his audience views the political world. His objective is neither a total and immediate conversion by any and all means, nor a defense of a particular set of policies. Instead the theorist attempts to demonstrate by reference to familiar examples, the advantages that follow from substituting for the accepted ways of viewing politics another mode of interpretation. In Wolin's opinion, when the theorist turns commentator, he does not become untheoretical. Nor does he simply appeal to perspectives derived from a conventional way of viewing politics. Rather, in Wolin's phrase, he engages in the politics of perception.

In his paper, Wolin pays particular attention to that typical interpretation of the political system provided by professional commentators. These, he argues, engage in political education. In part, they assume the role of unofficial councilor to those making decisions; in part, that of teacher, who by tacit instruction tells citizens how to think about the political world. But Wolin finds such political education to be inherently flawed, for it is neither critical nor theoretical. It does not prompt citizens to view their political system as problematical, nor have the commentators themselves examined their own conceptions of politics, citizenship, or the citizen's relation to his government, economy, and society. Wolin believes that it is not the commentator's intention to galvanize citizens into action. Rather he aims, whether intentionally or not, "to keep them gently oscillating between resignation and hope." The commentator uncritically accepts the existing state of affairs as given.

Not all political commentators project the same view of a situation, yet they all perform the same task within the same framework of the mass media. Because the media are an important part of the political economy, commentators seldom criticize their role and influence. In short, professional commentators lack distance. They do not provide the sort of criticism that would bring into view the "hidden and troubling interconnections" between the official theory of any society and the "anomalies, or manifest evils which the society wishes to deny, conceal, or explain away."

What is Wolin's alternative? First, he asserts that, in political commentary as in political theory, it is necessary to develop at least two conflicting principles of interpretation. Like Taylor, Wolin stresses the irreducible and necessary role of interpretation in theorizing about politics. Yet Wolin's stress falls, as Taylor's does not, upon the relationship between politics and vision (the title of Wolin's best-known book).[38] Although he is interested in the use of language and its relationship to actual practices and action, Wolin's framework is not that of analytical philosophy, the philosophy of science, moral philosophy, jurisprudence, Marxism, or existentialism. Wolin has extracted his own distinctive position from the history of political thought.

Political theory, as Wolin conceives it, is a critical vision that also provides a glimpse of how, from the existing state of affairs, a better social order and a more authentic life could be constructed. As in Marković's formulation, critique contains an implicit theory that must be made explicit. For this reason, a critical political theory must precede political commentary. The theorist ought to engage in commentary, and this for two reasons: one public and the other personal and intellectual. As a citizen, theorists ought to play a part in political education. They ought also to test their own general ideas to see whether they can make sense of the political world. If successful, they can help other citizens to perceive familiar political phenomena differently so that they become capable of seeing the abuses that exist and their relationship to the official principles of the society. Properly done, political commentary becomes more than the application of theory to practical concerns. It may turn into a legitimate enterprise in its own right.

Although Wolin, like Dworkin and Walzer, seeks to define a new role for political theory, he differs from both of them in his conception of what that might be. Dworkin wishes to find a standard for governmental action based on political principles rather than public policy. Walzer wishes political theorists to develop a practical, casuistical discipline to train citizens and decision-makers how to apply their moral principles to hard cases. Wolin, on the other hand, believes that it suffices to study alternative political theories and apply them to criticism of political arrangements. In this way citizens can develop the capacity to question the general views of their society, and to grasp its actual conditions with that degree of accuracy requisite to effective political action.

Wolin seems to doubt Walzer's supposition that all people share moral views derived from social practices that are an irreducible part of existing conditions for action and judgment. Although Wolin does not regard criticism of existing standards as the only task of political theory, he doubts the efficacy of any theory that does not call existing arrangements and practices into question. He thus challenges the vicarious political decision-making that in Walzer's view underlies the democratic process and is essential to voting and public opinion.

Clearly, to his earlier formulation of political theory as vision, Wolin has added a version of critical theory. Like Marković, he does not confine his critique to capitalist societies in general, or to American society in particular. For it is Wolin's argument that all societies have produced and indeed must produce systematically anomalies that run counter to whatever the official theory may be. But this raises the question of how a theorist deals with a vision alternative to his own, or to another reading of the text provided by a society with its statement of principles, institutions, and practices.

This problem, with which Taylor has dealt, becomes crucial whenever there emerge contested readings of politics and society. We need some examples and demonstrations of the principles operative in a political science or sociology based on contested concepts, or critical theory, or the politics of perception. Wolin apparently conceives of political commentary as an activity carried on by a political theorist who, without intermediate principles, applies trained vision to particular cases. Wolin needs to specify how this is to be done, particularly when, as Walzer stresses, there are conflicting principles that need to be taken into account.

Wolin, Dworkin, and Walzer agree that political theory can make significant contributions to political life. The political education of ordinary citizens and of political leaders is incomplete without some training in political theory. Where these three authors differ is in their conception of what specific role political theory ought to play in actual politics. Each has his own set of objectives and priorities, and these are not easy to harmonize. That such alternatives are available is evidence of the richness and diversity of political theory at this time.

1. Perhaps the best known statement was that by Peter Laslett. The successive volumes of *Philosophy, Politics and Society* contain a continuing commentary on this text. It occurs in *Philosophy, Politics and Society* (Second Series), ed. Peter Laslett and W. G. Runciman (Oxford: Blackwell, 1962).

2. T. D. Weldon, *The Vocabulary of Politics* (London: Penguin Books, 1953).

3. Alasdair MacIntyre, *A Short History of Ethics* (New York: Macmillan, 1966), pp. 264–65.

4. Alan Montefiore and Bernard Williams, eds., *British Analytical Philosophy* (London: Routledge, 1966).

5. J.G.A. Pocock, *The Machiavellian Moment: Florentine Political Thought and the Atlantic Republican Tradition* (Princeton, N. J.: Princeton University Press, 1975).

6. Bernard Williams, "A Critique of Utilitarianism," in J.J.C. Smart and Bernard Williams, *Utilitarianism for and against* (Cambridge: Cambridge University Press, 1973), p. 149.

7. MacIntyre, *A Short History of Ethics*, p. 267.

8. Charles Taylor, *Hegel* (Cambridge: Cambridge University Press, 1975).

9. Williams, "A Critique of Utilitarianism," p. 79.

10. *Ibid.*, p. 93.

11. Michael Walzer, *Just and Unjust Wars* (New York: Basic Books, 1977).

12. Williams, "A Critique of Utilitarianism," p. 93.

13. Taylor, *Hegel*.

14. Charles Taylor, *The Explanation of Behaviour* (New York: Humanities Press, 1964).

15. John Passmore, *A Hundred Years of Philosophy* (Baltimore: Pen-

guin, 1978), p. 530. Cited by Richard J. Bernstein, *Praxis and Action* (Philadelphia: University of Pennsylvania Press, 1971), p. 235.

16. Charles Taylor, "Neutrality in Political Science," in *Philosophy, Politics and Society* (Third Series), ed. Peter Laslett and W. G. Runciman (Oxford, 1969).

17. Taylor, "Neutrality in Political Science," p. 40.

18. Peter Winch, *The Idea of a Social Science and its Relation to Philosophy* (London: Routledge, 1958); A. R. Louch, *Explanation and Human Action* (Berkeley: University of California Press, 1969).

19. Charles Taylor, "Interpretation and the Sciences of Man," *Review of Metaphysics* 25 (1971), pp. 3-51.

20. *Ibid.*, 3 et seq.

21. *Ibid.*, p. 48.

22. Perhaps the best philosophical statements are by Ernest Nagel, *The Structure of Science* (London: Routledge, 1961) and Carl G. Hempel, *Philosophy of Science* (Englewood Cliffs, N. J.: Prentice-Hall, 1966).

23. I have profited considerably from an excellent article by David A. Crocker, "Marković's Concept of *Praxis* as Norm," *Inquiry* 20 (1977), 3-43, as well as from Richard J. Bernstein, *Praxis and Action*, op. cit. and *The Restructuring of Social and Political Theory* (New York: Harcourt Brace Jovanovich, 1976).

24. Bernstein, *Praxis and Action*, ix-xii.

25. Two books available in English translation by Marković are: *From Affluence to Praxis: Philosophy and Social Criticism* (Ann Arbor: University of Michigan Press, 1974), and *The Contemporary Marx: Essays on Humanist Communism* (Nottingham, 1974).

26. Leo Strauss, *What is Political Philosophy* (Glencoe, Ill.: The Free Press, 1959).

27. *Ibid.*, 27. See also Bloom's moving memorial to Professor Strauss in *Political Theory* 2 (1974), 371-92.

28. Op. cit., fn. 5.

29. J.G.A. Pocock, *Politics, Language, and Time* (New York: Atheneum, 1971), pp. 14-15.

30. J.G.A. Pocock, ed., *The Political Works of James Harrington* (Cambridge: Cambridge University Press, 1977).

31. Walzer, *Just and Unjust Wars*, fn. 11.

32. *Ibid.*, p. xv.

33. MacIntyre, *A Short History of Ethics*, p. 266.

34. Walzer, *Just and Unjust Wars*, p. xiii.

35. *Ibid.*, pp. xvi–xvii.

36. Ronald Dworkin, *Taking Rights Seriously* (Cambridge, Mass.: Harvard University Press, 1977).

37. *Ibid.*, p. 22.

38. Sheldon Wolin, *Politics and Vision* (Boston: Little Brown, 1960).

tive at least in the sense that first-order moral and political disagreement with the author can relevantly motivate disagreement with his philosophy, and impure in the sense that materials from non-philosophical sources—an involvement with history or the social sciences, for instance—is likely to play a more than illustrative part in the argument.

Analytical philosophy at that time wanted, and tried hard, to be neither normative nor impure. The distinction of fact and value (or rather, in this sort of case, of theory and value) supposedly served to segregate the philosophical.from the normative, while the companion distinction of analytic and synthetic served to segregate the philosophical from the historical or social-scientific. Granted this program, and granted the hereditary characteristics of political philosophy, analytical philosophy was bound not to do much for it. So explanation of the torpor of political philosophy at that time cannot just settle back on the characteristics of the time; it must, further, explain why political philosophy is peculiarly resistant to being made pure and non-normative, and why analytical philosophy at that point had those negative ambitions.

The first question I shall discuss, rather obliquely, below. The second question I shall not try to answer at all, but I will outline what an answer would have to explain. It is often suggested that the negative ambitions of analytical philosophy followed solely from its acceptance, in strong forms, of the two distinctions which I have mentioned, in particular the fact-value distinction. But this must be wrong. For even granted a sharp distinction between fact and value, one has to add a doctrine about the proper role of philosophy in order to determine that philosophy will concern itself with the one but not the other. This point is well illustrated by the work of one of the modern fathers of the fact-value distinction in analytical philosophy, G. E. Moore. Moore, having announced in *Principia Ethica* (Cambridge: Cambridge University Press, 1903) the existence of the so-called "naturalistic fallacy" and its consequence that no purely logical process could get one from metaphysical propositions to value judgments, was not at all deterred from giving up much of his book to reports of what, in his view, was good. Of course, granted the naturalistic fallacy, these remarks must be in effect additional to his metaphysical and logical claims, but he does not mind making them. He differs from his successors not in views about the relationship of metaphysics or logic to statements of value, but on whether books written by philosophers should confine themselves to metaphysics and logic.

In part this difference can be traced to a difference about the epistemology of value judgments. There might be some reason, if an obscure one, to suppose that if the discovery of what was good rested, as Moore supposed, on the intuition of non-natural properties, then a philosopher would have some appropriate skill of holding relevant intellectual items in transparent suspension in his mind—a skill not peculiar to philosophy but at least favored by it. But once the later developments of fact-value theory led to non-cognitive accounts of the holding of value judgments, then indeed there was a difficulty about the philosopher's claim, so far as value judgments are concerned, on anyone's attention. In particular, the tendency to regard value judgments (or rather, their overt utterance) as primarily protreptic, as seeking to exhort or command their hearers, leaves a special darkness about the relation between the philosopher who says such things and his audience.

There has been a real problem about the relation of the modern moral or political philosopher to his audience, of what claim he has on anyone's attention, and I shall come back to it, briefly, at the end of this paper—though in a context, I hope, less flatly discouraging than that presented by the sort of view I have just mentioned. But in the present connection, it is important that the limitations on analytical philosophy could not possibly have been imposed merely by the fact-value distinction in itself. They required also a special view of the responsibilities of philosophy. It is important, too, that the limitations on philosophy, and the associated drying-up of political philosophy, were not uniquely encouraged by the belief, no doubt important to many "end of ideology" views, that serious value disagreement was at an end and substantial consensus obtained. On the contrary, it was precisely a sense of the contrast between the plurality of values, and their unresolvable conflict, as opposed to the supposed universality of logic and science, that helped to motivate the fact-value distinction.

The fact-value distinction and how to see it in 3-D. I mentioned the question of why political philosophy could not throw off its hereditary involvement with the normative and the impure and form a pure but productive alliance with the chastely limited ambitions of analytical philosophy. The short answer is that the peculiarly two-dimensional operation of the fact-value distinction as then employed offered all it had to offer about ethics or about value *in general*, and left nothing interesting to be said about the distinctively political issues. The distinction imposed a contrast between those elements of language which registered the state of the world, and those that expressed policies, principles, or decisions to change it—or, at any rate, in another version, affective reactions which related to desires to change it. Many of our most interesting value concepts evidently combined both these functions, serving both to register some complex set of facts and to express an evaluation. But the evaluation had to be logically separable from the facts, or a certain way of describing the world would itself import evaluations. Fact would entail value, and, most basically, a certain kind of freedom which this view demands—that an individual's values should not be dictated to him by the world—would have been abrogated.

If this were right, then it would follow that nothing of a very interesting philosophical character could be said about these complex value concepts. Philosophy would make its general point about the separateness of the value element, and the question of why the descriptive elements should be grouped together, and how the evaluations related to a broader context of beliefs, would be left to the social sciences and thus, by the purity requirement, definitively outside philosophy. From this point of view, the complex value concept cannot invite the question of how those facts involve those values. That presumably would be a philosophical question, were it possible, but from this perspective it is not possible. No fact involves value. We, or other societies, apply values to some facts; and the questions invited by the complex value concept can only be how, and when, and to what facts we or they apply value, and that is seen as a question for the social sciences. But now the distinctive subject matter of political philosophy must certainly involve complex value concepts, for it is not any old right and wrong, but that imported by lawfulness, or justice, or equality, or liberty, which are its concerns. Hence the two-dimensional fact-value theory could find nothing of interest for political philosophy, and it is not an accident that political philosophy should have preserved its old recalcitrance in that respect.

Nor, equally, that it should remain impure. For if there is to be a philosophical way of doing better respect to the complexity of these value concepts and their relations to a wider background, it will not be one which totally leaves behind the interests of the social sciences, but rather cooperates with them. I certainly do not want to try to give here any extensive suggestions about the fact-value distinction and what should happen to it. But it is worth mentioning one possibility which curiously did not attract as much interest from fact-value theorists as it might have done: namely that there is no compulsion to use a given value concept at all. Two-dimensional fact-value theory implied that for any mixed concept C it was always possible to have a concept C' which had all and only the descriptive content of C but lacked its evaluative force; and that it would be a non-philosophical question whether C' had a use. But we can take it as itself a philosophical consideration that C could lose both its identity and its point without its evaluative force; and that its identity, further, can be involved in its relations to a wider range of concepts. By emphasizing this consideration, one might hope to recognize that evaluations can be more intimately bound up with ways of describing the world than the earlier analytical account would allow, so that, for instance, the selection of certain kinds of conduct for evaluation itself makes sense only in terms of a general framework of beliefs; and yet one could at the same time preserve the truth that moral beliefs cannot just be a record of what the world is like, and even, with a certain difference, preserve that ultimate value-freedom which the fact-value theorist wanted.

The concept of *sin*, for instance, relates in itself fact and value, and relates them in a complex way so that they are not merely external to each other—one could not merely have all those beliefs and abandon those values—but, as modern life reveals, there is no necessity for human beings to use the concept of sin. On this way of looking at it, one can regain the three-dimensional sense that it is in the context of a set of beliefs about the world and society that values have a meaning; one can examine the detailed structure of a set of values of this kind without supposing that it is the only possible one; one can approach the value systems of other times and places with a more realistic and flexible set of categories; and one will need to, and be able to, make better use of the social sciences than to regard them as the repository of the non-philosophical.[1]

It is only with a certain difference that this preserves the requirement of ultimate value-freedom. The idea that one could, so to speak, withdraw one's value commitment from a complex value term presumably would mean, if it meant anything, that one had a peculiarly individual kind of freedom; but with the recognition that values are more deeply incorporated in systems of belief, the freedom in question becomes more ultimate and less available, since the reconstruction of an entire outlook has less the appearance of being to hand. The freedom becomes the freedom of man rather than of men. But it was only the extreme abstraction of the earlier view which gave the impression of anything else. It is interesting that the purest exponent of the earlier kind of analytical view I have been discussing, R. M. Hare, has now moved to a much more normative stance, but it is one, of utilitarian type, which precisely preserves the individualism implicit in the earlier view, and, at the same time, the opinion that substantive complex value concepts are in principle redundant or uninteresting.

Reflexive social understanding. It is possible to see that type of element in analytical philosophy as ideological—not, perhaps, in the sense that its propagation serves an interest, but at least in the sense that its direction and presuppositions are formed in ways not evident from its surface, and perhaps not evident to the writers themselves, and which admit of social explanation. I do not want to discuss the question of which, if any, such explanations are true: they tend in fact to wander between the vague and the anecdotal. But I should like to suggest that at any rate analytical philosophy up to now has been notably ill-equipped among philosophies for considering whether such things might be true, for reflexively raising questions of its own relations to social reality. The extreme abstraction I have already referred to, and the conceptual character of its subject matter, not only in an obvious way set it apart from considerations of this kind, but actually logically exclude them. An epistemological reflexion, in purely conceptual terms, on the status of theses of analytical philosophy is of course available and has taken up only too much attention; but reflexion in concrete historical terms was excluded by the ban on the empirical.

Insofar as the purely conceptual stance helps this immunity to social reflexion, one might hope that a greater openness to the impurities of the social sciences might help. Indeed it might, in an obvious and immediate sense, in that much social science at this moment is obsessed with such issues, and some sociology gives the appearance of having collapsed into pure social epistemology. But if, in general terms, one were to believe that the mere presence of the social sciences were to encourage such reflexion, one would clearly be very optimistic, since some branches of the social sciences, in particular some types of political science, are the very subjects which have most emphatically invited complaints of lacking such reflexive self-criticism. It might be said that that criticism would be avoided if the idea of social understanding were joined to philosophy, since philosophy is essentially reflexive. But it is a marriage broker's optimism to suppose that the mating of reflexive philosophy with the consciousness of social reality gives reflexive social consciousness: as Bernard Shaw said to the actress, suppose it has your brains and my looks? To take a particular example, Winch's theory of the social sciences blends an openness to anthropological data with a philosophical method; indeed it obviously represents an over-close assimilation of social to conceptual understanding. But it is certainly not better blessed with reflexive consciousness than was either analytical philosophy or positivist social science.

There is in fact no mechanical way of ensuring that political and moral philosophers are more sensitive to these issues—as they should be, although the sensitivity should be prepared to take the form, on occasion, of looking the difficulty in the face and passing on (just as one's recognition of other traditions in philosophy should often take the form of looking them in the face and getting on with something one actually believes in). The lesson I draw from that is that the education of political philosophers should include such epistemological materials as will help them to get some measure of the varying claims of the sociology of knowledge. As it has been said that metaphysicians and philosophers of language should not be verificationists, but should have a verificationist conscience, so political philosophers should have a readiness to be embarrassed by the possibility of reflexion on the formation and direction of their views.

Bit-by-bit or systematic? The question of how systematic philosophy should be, and the related, if not identical, question of how far it should consist of theories, is one that has been the subject of much disagreement within analytical philosophy; with, extremely roughly, a British tradition of piecemeal improvisation (with the conspicuous exception of Russell) being opposed to a theory-directed Teutono-American tradition.

The present state of this question largely corresponds to the present political and economic fortunes of these two groupings, and it can hardly be doubted that the more systematic and theory-based approach has, in central areas of philosophy, simply won. In the philosophy of language, notably, the point has established itself that an isolated distinction or analysis lacks both sense and point: Austin's professed view, that one collects linguistic distinctions like types of beetles, can be seen to be absurd about linguistic distinctions, and not very clever about beetles.

In a theory of meaning such as Davidson's, as also in Quine's, the notion of theory itself plays a quite central role: for the notion of meaning is introduced (insofar as it *is* introduced—the point will do just as well with regard to the surrogates for meaning in these theories) essentially in terms of what conditions are associated with a given expression by the theory which optimally fits all observed utterances. Now what is being referred to here is of course an empirical theory, a theory which a linguist might form about a given language which he was trying to understand, but the point has further ramifications into philosophy itself: for the philosopher will try systematically to give analyses or elucidations of expressions of our own language which will be of a type to fit in, at least, with such an empirical theory, and without some such constraint the choice between possible analyses or elucidations of expressions becomes indeterminate and pointless. This is a strong example, but the same point can be argued to hold more generally; it is only in terms of what could be said about a lot of cases, or expressions, or areas, that the choice of what to say about *this* case becomes determinate. It is the absence of such constraints that makes a lot of Wittgensteinian philosophy so empty. The original view was that what made the choice of an elucidation or a philosophical remark determinately appropriate was a *concern*, and what makes a lot of Wittgenstein's later work impressive is the presence of a recognizable such concern—his own. But many of his followers seem to be addressing postulated or type-concerns, which represent at best only a very weak constraint on what is in fact very inexplicit theory.

The systematic constraints on the philosophy of language hold for other very general areas of philosophy: metaphysics, theory of knowledge, philosophy of mind; in some part, because they *do* hold for the philosophy of language. Without some such constraints—and I do not want to exaggerate the degree to which they are yet clear or agreed—it is hard to see why one philosophical remark should be more relevant than another, or what might count as an explanation. In this sense, vaguely as I have pointed to it, I should want to claim that philosophy should be systematic. Moral and political philosophy are also parts of philosophy. But it does not follow from that that we should necessarily have systematic moral and political philosophy; or at least, if it does follow, it follows only in the weak sense, which I accept, that these branches of philosophy should be responsive to systematic demands from elsewhere: for one thing, the grammar of moral and political sentences—literal grammar, not Wittgensteinian—is the same as that of other sentences. What does not follow is that moral and political philosophy should have their own systems, or that to supply system should be a primary demand on philosophers in these areas.

The reason is that an important aim, and certain consequence, of systematizing in these areas is to reduce or eliminate conflict among our ideas and sentiments; and before we set out doing that, and while we are doing it, we should reflect on the significance of conflict. Conflict in our moral sentiments and beliefs is, first, a historically, socially, and probably psychologically conditioned phenomenon, the product of such things as pluralistic societies and rapid cultural change as well as, perhaps, more generally distributed psychological needs which tend to conflict. We can, to some extent, understand *why* we have conflicting sentiments, but that does not mean, or should not mean, that we therefore withdraw our loyalty from them. Second, it is not true that any situation in which there is no such conflict is better than one in which

there is, or even—what is perhaps more plausible—that conflict reduction is an aim which always has a very strong prior-
ity. In the case of belief-conflict and of explanatory theories,
conflict-reduction is an undoubted aim: whether it be for the
pragmatist reason, that conflict-elimination itself defines the
aim of the explanatory endeavor, or for the realist reason that
conflicting beliefs cannot both, in some more substantial
sense, be true. But the articulation of our moral sentiments
does not necessarily obey these constraints, and to demand
that they be schooled by the requirement of system is to alter
our moral perception of the world, not just to make it in some
incontestable sense more rational.

This is what makes Rawls' model so misleading, which as-
similates moral "intuitions" to the intuitions of a native
speaker such as are the input to a linguistic theory. It is not
merely that more is involved in schooling the moral responses, in "reflective equilibrium," to theory than there is in
finally writing off some marginal utterances as deviant. It is
that the role of theory is different. It is the role of linguistic
theory to explain and predict acceptable utterances, and it is
the theory for doing that. But in the case of moral sentiments,
a Rawlsian theory, that is to say a set of principles or moral
notions which unifies our moral opinions and in that sense
predicts the reflective reaction to a possible or imaginary case,
is not alone in the field: for we can understand equally an external theory, e.g. of social explanation, which predicts that
no one set of such principles or notions will do the job. Thus
we may have systematically conflicting sentiments, for instance, about the value of character and the value of particular
actions and intentions; or of the value of particular, non-
moral, sentiments and the value of moral, impersonal sentiments of justice. We can feel the force of both utilitarian and
anti-utilitarian arguments. Moreover, we can see perhaps
why we have these conflicting sentiments; and if so, we cannot agree that whether there must be a unified theory which
"predicts" the response to various situations, in the Rawlsian
way, or else that some of our responses are to be jettisoned.

There are in fact two different points to be made here. First, the mere fact of the possibility of external explanation of value-conflict means that the Rawlsian question parallel to the question in the philosophy of language, "What unified and systematic set of principles will 'predict' these reactions?" is a question which need not necessarily have an answer. The unity of a language—even the unity of *my* language—is given in relation to the explanatory theory itself: whereas the unity of my values or sentiments is not so given, and in relation to the external explanations of how I came by them, they may emerge as not unified. (A man between two cultures is not like an effective speaker of a Creole language.)

The second point is that when these conflicts become clear to a man, there is still a question of to what extent and how he should reduce them. Thus many of us now have two kinds of sentiments about questions of people being killed: utilitarian sentiments on the one hand, and on the other sentiments which have a complex articulation but which involve such notions as that with regard to who is to get killed, no choice is better than choice, and that if a choice has to be made, structural considerations (such as fewer rather than more, the already dying rather than those not already dying, etc.) take precedence. This conjunction of sentiments leads to conflict; and utilitarians in particular (a) argue for a rationalization of our outlook and (b) argue for its rationalization in the utilitarian direction, diagnosing the second set of sentiments as the residue of some earlier non-utilitarian outlook. But there are at least three levels at which this pressure for rationalization can be resisted.

First—and this is one which utilitarians themselves can recognize—the consequences involved in the actual social realization may be more extensive and more harmful than expected. Second, at a psychological level, the rationalized values may be harder to live with and to handle. And third— removed now from utilitarian concerns—it may be the case that these sentiments are metaphysically involved with more of our view of what people are than appears on the surface.

That requires exploration, and that exploration requires patience with our apparent irrationalities. And perhaps more than patience—at least, indefinite patience.

It is an open, and I think difficult, question how far it is an unquestionable ideal that even ultimately, moral responses should be harmoniously integrated, in ways in which ours now are for the most part certainly not. (A related, and equally difficult, question is how far an analogous demand holds on first-personal rationality: it is certainly a far from self-evident demand, made by Rawls, Nagel, and many other writers, that one should rationally plan for one's life *as a whole*, as though it were a given rectangle to be optimally filled in.) But whatever the answer to those questions, it is certain that such an ideal end is not to be taken as realized in the deep structure of our existing sentiments, nor to be approached by the direct route of setting out to school them in accordance with system. First they have to be understood, which, while it must be done in the context of a systematic philosophy in general, is likely to be a patient and untidy business.

It may be said that morality requires action, and action requires decision—one hopes, on rational principles. It is true that we have to act, but it is only the view that action exhausts the point and content of moral thought that could lead anyone to think that that is the end of this matter. What follow rather are such familiar facts as that sometimes we act, and necessarily act, with less than 100 percent conviction; or again—less familiar, this, than the well-known liberal lack of conviction, and perhaps more invigorating—that it is possible to act with 100 percent conviction on one occasion while quite conscious that on another occasion, only obscurely different from that first one, conviction might not have arrived. The relations between action, conviction, and rationality is an area in which moral philosophy, the philosophy of mind, and metaphysics, most significantly meet.

But however that may be, politics, it may reasonably be said, is a different matter: for while individual persons can to varying extents go round with conflicting moral sentiments, there is a demand of rational consistency and principle in public positions (quite apart from what is legally enacted). There is obvious truth in this; but among many further things that should be said about it are two which, in terms of a program for political philosophy, qualify its effect. First, the requirement of consistency in principle which obtains on a series of public decisions by an enduring authority in a rational state (idealized as that may be), or on the program of one party (even more idealized though that may be), it obviously does not extend to political life as a whole, which precisely can embody not only conflicts of interests, and of straightforwardly opposed principles, but of conflicting values, and of conflicting interpretations of the same values (consider here the conflicts of equality of opportunity with equality of esteem; or of justice as equality with justice as entitlement). The philosopher's thoughts do not have to be directed to solving these differences; he may do his best work, in fact, in sharpening them, by making it clear in what ways both have a foot in our sentiments. This may not be, in the short term at least, an altogether helpful activity, but it can be a good one.

Second, even insofar as a philosopher's efforts are directed to assisting rationality in political practice, they may helpfully take the form of providing structures in which it can be recognized how much conflict of value that process can and should absorb. In particular I have in mind here the philosophical study of decision theory, with particular emphasis on structures more complex than the linear, often utilitarian, models, with an emphasis on direct comparability of values, which have often prevailed. It is admitted that actual structures of decision in political bodies lie a long way from these idealizations; but it is also probable that very simple models of what practical rationality is can feed into and affect decision processes. A combination of a mastery of the appropriate formal skills and a steady sense of the existence of genuinely competing and only partially reconcilable goods—something which distinguishes the work of Amartya Sen in this field—is something which political philosophy needs to provide.

History. I am not going to say anything, except by implication, about genuine historical understanding. I suppose, for reasons which are obvious and would be tedious to rehearse, that genuine historical understanding is of the first importance in the understanding of politics and political thought; that diachronic distancing is one very important form of the distancing we need to secure from our own society; that that gains another importance when the society is an ancestor of our own. Further, it seems to me that to read Plato only as in last week's *Mind* is to lose an important part of reading Plato.

About what genuine historical understanding of a text is, understanding of what it *meant*, I agree with Quentin Skinner that if it is recoverable at all, it must be in the kind of terms which he has detailed, of those contemporary expectations in terms of which a communicative intention could be realized. Moreover, it is clear beyond doubt that the fundamental sense of the question, asked of a historical text, "what does it mean?" is "what *did* it mean?"

However, there is another sort of question, which can be expressed in such forms as "What does it mean to me?" or "What do I get out of it?" This question, I would rather say, is not so much asked *of* the text, as asked *about* it: and that is asked about a book, a set of words, which maximally resemble the words written in the past. These questions, and the answers we give to them, seem to me only rather loosely connected with history, in the sense of the past which gave rise to the book, but they have quite a lot to do with the *history of the book*—in particular, the more interesting among these questions may continue that history. The book's *Nachleben* is not only itself studied, it is lived.

When we treat these books in this way, and for instance represent arguments in them in our own terms, supply modern questions which are like what we take these questions to be, and so on, we are doing something which is indeed conventionally called "history of philosophy," but is really a sort of philosophy—we might call it "history-of-philosophy philosophy." In particular, we should beware of two misleading impressions that may be created by calling it "history of philosophy." One is that the pursuit of the maximally consistent interpretation—a basic rule of this kind of exercise—is a genuine principle of historical reconstruction. We may think it is, for instance, because of its resemblance to a type of principle that plays a genuine role in the sort of linguistic theory I discussed earlier: the principle of charity, by which one interprets an alien language so that what should be evidently true to native speakers comes out as true, and they don't simply contradict themselves. But that principle, at that level of generality, plays a different role: it is not just a contingent assumption, for we have no independent control over the idea that in general they might be evidently mistaken or contradicting themselves (really). In the case of a particular author and a particular text, however, there is in principle more control over this idea, and some conclusions about it can even be reached *a priori*. Thus people spend enormous time (I have spent some myself) on trying to find interpretations of Plato's *Sophist* which make Plato's theories consistent. But if Plato's *Sophist* is about what we think it is about (and granted his theories about these very difficult subjects came when they did) it is wildly improbable that his theories on those subjects would succeed in being consistent. Of course, the rejection of the principle of consistent interpretation leaves the whole question in a very boring state, since then there are no unique solutions and there are indeterminately many ways in which it might be inconsistent. But to count boringness as a criticism—of answers, I mean, not of questions—just shows that one is doing philosophy, or at any rate, not history.

The second misleading consequence of taking the history of philosophy, in the usual sense, as history, is that we think we have a rationale for doing it; for instance, in the sense of providing ourselves with the historical background of our own ideas. But if the study is not genuinely history, then it doesn't provide us with the historical background to anything. These texts, of ancient provenance, bearing some largely indeterminate relation in our understanding to what they meant, are complex but ambiguous objects on which we project sets of philosophical ideas rather different in content from those we would be exercising in our own person. It may be interesting, helpful, instructive, even in some ways tell us about the past, but our justification for doing it, if there is one, can only very complexly be related to the fact that these men said what they said with certain meanings in the past. History of philosophy, and in particular, history of political philosophy, can, in principle, be made into history; but as it is most often done, especially in the spirit of analytical philosophy, it must be defended, if it is defensible, as a funny kind of philosophy with archaizing elements (something in the style of Stravinsky's *Pulcinella*), rather than as irresponsible history.

CONCLUSION

I have touched, broadly, on a number of themes. I have implied, without saying, that the political philosopher must be in touch with moral philosophy, and have said that, freed from the narrower preoccupations of the fact-value distinction, he will have the opportunity and the need to study substantial complex value notions, not merely in their conceptual interrelations, narrowly conceived, but in the background of beliefs and non-moral conceptions which give them sense; and that in this, his work must certainly interrelate closely with that of the social sciences. I have suggested that his work may require now a particular kind of reflexive sensitivity which is likely to be assisted by a study of epistemological issues in relation to the social sciences: and one may add, the natural sciences, too. He should have a sense of the systematic demands of philosophy without demanding a system within moral or political philosophy themselves; and he should help in some respects to keep alive the sense of genuine moral conflicts, the origins of which we may well understand, but which are prone to be prematurely rationalized out of existence. One area in which he may usefully be able to do this is the development of more complex and realistic structures in decision theory.

This leaves the question which so bothered many analytical philosophers of the fact-value persuasion: By what right can a philosopher claim the attention of an audience on these themes, especially if—as I, certainly, have taken for granted —his concerns will be in some part normative? It seems to me an encouraging sign of how far philosophy has come in the past fifteen or even ten years, that this question, which seemed so honestly pressing at one time, should seem so boring now. For its answer clearly is that he has whatever claim any adult and reflective person may have on the attention of others if he has thoughts about some important subject. He can sacrifice that claim, or fail to deliver on it, in as many ways as there are of writing words which are dead, unimaginative, stupid, ill-informed, and so forth. Being a philosopher, his claim to attention is likely to be, as always, more weighted towards the end of subtle analysis and the fact that some of his claims follow from others, than for instance, to lie in a wide and seasoned experience of men and events; but to suppose that that is all and only what should be asked of him, is from all points of view idiotic.

In saying that, and throughout, I have in mind still one who is doing analytical philosophy. I have spoken critically of some earlier limitations of the genre, but as I said at the beginning, I do not think that reform has changed or will change it out of all recognition. It would be pointless and unhelpful now, any more than at the beginning, to say what I take its defining characteristics to be, if indeed it has definite bounds. I take a generous view of it, but certainly much which is called philosophy is excluded. It is cheering that in political philosophy it has survived its regeneration into something interesting, with its undoubted virtues intact. In its insistence, at its best, on the values of unambiguous statement and recognizable argument; its patience; its lack of contempt for the familiar; its willingness to meet with the formal and natural sciences; its capacity for genuine and discussable progress—in all this, and despite its many and often catalogued limitations, it remains the only real philosophy there is.

1. This is to imply that the study of the conceptual interrelations of a group's outlook forms part of the social scientific study of that group. It does not imply that it forms more than part. The idea that social science is, more than everything else, conceptual investigation (cf. Winch) is a quite different, and to me unacceptable, position.

THE PHILOSOPHY OF
THE SOCIAL SCIENCES

CHARLES TAYLOR

In what way is the philosophy of science relevant in the training of political philosophers? Or, if this sounds grandiose, of
people who take courses in political theory in order better to
understand and judge the political reality around them?

The aim of this training should be to make accessible to
students a number of different languages through which political things can be described and assessed; and this means both
making them more aware of the terms underlying their present unreflecting judgments and descriptions, making them
thus more articulate, but also making them bi- and trilingual,
so that they can begin to see the limitation and the historically
conditioned nature of any philosophical language, and more
particularly of languages of political philosophy.

How does this relate to the issues of the philosophy of science? Different languages of political reality, incorporating
different conceptions of what politics and the political are, are
related to different notions of what it is to study politics;
hence, to what is political science. This is evident. The same
notion of the political can be put in terms of political ontology—propositions concerning political reality—or in terms
of statements about the science of politics.

But philosophy of science has a special importance in that
our modern philosophical tradition has been so oriented to
epistemology that reflective philosophical conceptions of
what politics is have frequently been formulated out of a spoken or unspoken concern for politics as an object of study.
This might seem at first sight a startling observation, since the

main interest behind reflective formulations about the nature of politics down through the ages has surely been the rectification of political practice. But an important stream of Enlightenment thought has built the scientific study of politics into the ideal of a rectified practice. The political order can be set aright if we study it as an object in nature like those others which mechanics has so successfully mapped, and then restructure it according to our findings.

Those who stand in this tradition hold in fact to the view that the proper categories in which to understand the political are those by which it becomes amenable to a scientific study which follows certain paradigm procedures, notably those derived from the physical sciences. What is to be considered political reality depends in the end on what can be studied by certain procedures. Or at least, so the opponents of this way of thinking about politics claim, and, I believe, with some justice. And even if the extreme claim is not justified against the heirs of Enlightenment science, that they have cut their view of the political to their methodological cloth, there is still a complex enough interpenetration of epistemological and practical motives underlying our adoption of one or another language of politics, that the attempt to be philosophically multilingual has to be carried on, among other ways by a study of certain issues in the philosophy of science.

When people begin to be reflective about the political in our civilization, there is a view of politics which tends to come to the fore, and which they have trouble freeing themselves, from even if they find it unsatisfactory. This view could be called, for short, the instrumental one. Political institutions and practices are to be understood as instruments to the attainment of certain ends.

The notion of an instrument, of course, refers us implicitly to that of a subject who is capable of deploying this instrument, whether or not the nature of this subject is thematically described. The subject underlying the instrumentalist view of politics is the individual or group, where "group" refers to a segment of a society, not to the whole.

Now the nature of an instrument is that it serves some goal definable without reference to that instrument. An instrument serves to bring about an end with which the proper wielding of the instrument is in causal relation; hence the two: end-state and appropriate use of instrumental, are independently definable.

In keeping with the modern age's conceptions of the primacy of the subject, the goals of individuals and groups are thought of as taken up by them, rather than being determined by the nature of things, and hence are called by the modern term "values." The political process is then seen as instrumental in implementing or frustrating these values. We can thus think of politics, for instance, as "the authoritative allocation of values for a society." Or we think of the political system as one which receives inputs and produces outputs. The inputs include the independently identified "demands"; the outputs fulfil or frustrate them.

What does this conception screen out? Any view of the political community, its structures and practices, where what is important is the quality of common life they embody. For instance let us think as an example of an Aristotle-derived notion of politics, where what is significant is the quality of common deliberation. On this view, to sketch it briefly, political society is a society whose members are subject to law and to authoritative decisions, where these decisions emerge in some way which takes account of the deliberation of (many) citizens about the advantageous and the harmful, the just and the unjust, where the common deliberation weighs for something in the outcome. A régime is not political in this use of the term where men live under an authority whose decisions take no account of their deliberation, or where the issues up for decision are decided by a process that takes no account of common deliberation, e.g., by who has how many tanks in the main square at sun-up.

Now the instrumentalist conception can construct something like the distinction between political and despotic régimes: its own variant of that distinction, in which the process of political decision takes account of the "values," or "demands" of those concerned. But this cannot capture what is of importance to the Aristotle-derived view above. For what this stresses is *deliberation*. It is not enough for this purpose that a given régime take account of my values, which it might do without any thought or action on my part, pursuing some law of anticipated reaction; what is important is that I play a part in a common deliberation. This because deliberating about the advantageous and the harmful, the just and the unjust is (in part) how we acquire a characteristically human excellence, as well as being involved in the exercise of this virtue, which is practical wisdom. Thus for a political régime, there must be some degree of common deliberation; and these regimes, further, can be assessed on what kind of issues are the matter of their common deliberation: are they mainly concerned, for instance, with what economic policies will ensure a high rate of growth of GNP? Or are questions raised about the ends of life, and about how society should be ordered so as to further these ends differently conceived? It is clear that if common deliberation is important because it furthers and expresses practical wisdom, then the latter type of society will be thought superior.

We can see now why this Aristotle-derived view of society is irreducible to the terms of the instrumentalist conception. For the political process cannot be understood as an instrument in relation to ends which are independently defined. What is important about it is the degree to which it embodies a common deliberation, and of what quality (over what issue, how clairvoyant, how free from hypocrisy, cant, cliché, bad faith, lies, dissimulations, deceptions, and the other standard blemishes of political life). And this is important because deliberation is the exercise and hence nurture of practical wisdom. But neither of these relations is instrumental. Proper deliberation is not a means to practical wisdom, it is the exercise of it seen as a virtue, i.e., a disposition. Proper deliberation is thus part of the end sought; as it issues from and sustains practical wisdom, it is the end. Similarly, the political process cannot be seen as a means to deliberation; it either embodies common deliberation or it does not; or it embodies deliberation of this quality or that. The question here is the extent to which the political process is, among other things, a deliberative process.

Those who want to raise questions about political régimes and the quality of political life are unable to do so as long as they remain within the terms of the instrumentalist conception. These reflections are very hard to raise in modern polities, and in the modern university as well. Most people understand quite well references to different qualities of community life, be it in face-to-face groups where, for instance, the atmosphere of a gathering is strained or friendly; or in society as a whole, which may have an atmosphere of community and mutual help, or, on the contrary, estrangement, mistrust, and lack of mutual recognition. Indeed, some societies seem to be moving from the first state to the second, and people are acutely aware of this decline. The atmosphere, the quality of community life, is deteriorating, they say.

But this is then interpreted in the terms of the instrumentalist conception, which as we saw, is also an atomist conception, starting from individuals or partial groups. Community spirit or community thought is accounted for by "consensus," the convergence of individual conceptions, or majority emotional responses. Individuals influence and affect each other in their responses, and are influenced and affected by the majority response, but the ontology we are dealing with is that of individuals (or partial groups). Community atmosphere cannot be given a holistic interpretation.

And thus when we come to institutions, these are understood instrumentally. Certain institutions or political practices are seen to affect the community spirit or atmosphere in certain ways. For instance, it may be thought that a community center will favor "interaction" (another term of our social science which fairly shrieks out its atomistic assumptions) and thus improve community spirit by changing the attitudes of large numbers of individuals. But it is much harder for people to conceive how certain institutions or practices may embody a certain quality of community spirit; for this would give a reality to community spirit, as embodied in these common institutions, which would have to be understood holistically, and not interpreted as the joint product of individual attitudes or reactions.

Thus certain social distinctions, such as that between welfare recipients and others, both in the way they are drawn, and in how they are commonly understood, may express and entrench a certain degree of solidarity and its absence, which degree cannot itself be understood in terms of a concatenation of individual attitudes, but is rather the common background and object of reference in relation to which individuals form attitudes.

To talk of institutions and practices as embodying in this sense the spirit of a community or a certain quality of common deliberation breaks in two respects with the ontology underlying the atomist-instrumentalist conception. First, it allows that there are common actions, emotions, dispositions of spirit, and the like which cannot be broken down into concatenations of states of individuals. In other words, it holds that psychological predicates do not all apply primarily to individuals. The distinction between the public and the private, for instance, which is important for a certain tradition of political thought that comes down to us from the ancients, can be made only if we allow such common states into our ontology. The public—what is in the public realm, as against the private—cannot be accounted for by the number of people aware of it, for it may be generally known that p, even thought p is not in the public realm; nor by some recursive function, of the form: all know that p, and each knows that the others know that p, and each knows, etc.; for this, too could be satisfied without p's being in the public realm. Something is in the public realm, when it is a common object, as defined by the public life of the society. Its being in the public realm is a status it enjoys in virtue of being a common object, where this is irreducible to its being an object for me, for you, for A, B, C, etc.

Of course, something being in the public realm may be partly a matter of convention; e.g., a motion moved in Parliament is an event in the public realm. But then the distinction of what is public and what is private gives official recognition to what is and ought to be a common object in a paradigm way, as against what is only accidentally so. But this the modern view must misinterpret either in terms of who knows about it, or of who is concerned, or in terms of responsibility: What the MP does concerns us and we are responsible for it; it engages us, and hence is in the public realm. But the original sense bound all these aspects together.

Only if one admits such common states can one see practices and institutions as embodying them. But if practices and institutions can embody common states, then they have to be the kind of realities that can be understood in an expressive and not just in an instrumental dimension. So that once we break with the instrumentalist conception, we can see the institutions and practices of a given society as offering, as it were, a vocabulary in which different common states can be expressed. Let me try to make this point a little clearer. Given institutions and practices define certain ways of acting, and these actions presuppose certain notions about human being, society, perhaps also the extrahuman environment, and the relations between them, without which these actions would not make sense. Let us take the example of voting, as we see it in modern elections or in assemblies. Voting cannot just be characterized as the marking of ballots, placing of stones in an urn, moving levers on machines, or whatever. We cannot account for it without giving the point of the action; and that is to arrive at a social decision by concatenating individual decisions.

But this presupposes a certain notion of human beings and their relation to society if it is to make sense. It presupposes that normally human beings can or ought to come to a resolution about their will or preferences on their own. It presupposes, in other words, some notion of the individual will, otherwise the concatenation process doesn't make sense. And it implies as well that something can be called a social decision which arises in this way as a result of concatenating a whole lot of individual decisions.

There are a number of societies where both these conceptions would fall somewhere between the incomprehensible and the wicked. Traditional village societies, for instance, where decisions arise out of a non-concatenated consensus, where a topic is talked around until a consensus emerges. In these the notion of a partial will—a decision arrived at by A which abstracted entirely from the common bent of the community—would appear as wicked; and the idea of the vote as a *social* decision process would appear madness, since how can there be a social decision by a procedure which dissolves the community?

Of course, even without the underlying conceptions of individual and social decision, we could have a procedure of marking ballots, or putting stones in an urn or whatever, but it would have a quite different meaning. A ritual of confirmation of certain leaders; or part of a struggle of rivalry of one tribe against another; or whatever. But the vote as a concatenating procedure of social decision requires these conceptions.

We can say that voting as a social procedure expresses these conceptions. This activity, fully understood—that is, with its point as well—offers a certain understanding of man and society. It can be thought even to overlap in function with a theoretical statement which might lay out that understanding of man, as this in turn might be thought to overlap with, let us say, a story encapsulate the same idea. For the practice is one which gives us this conception of man, that is, it becomes a conception for us if we engage in the practice with a full understanding of its point; and not in some other practice which borrows the same forms—like our "voting" as a ritual of confirmation of leadership above, which is analogous to us-

ing the same morpheme with another sense, an institutional
homonym, as it were.

It may even be that a conception is a conception for us in
virtue of being implicit in our social practices and institutions,
before we formulate these ideas conceptually—indeed, without our ever formulating them conceptually. This was the lot
of primitive societies, and of societies in our tradition before
the awakening of social theory. And it may be that now the
nuances of our conceptions of ourselves and our societies as
expressed in our practices and institutions are as yet inade-
quately expressed in our theoretical formulations. We might
say that in these cases, we have only implicit, semi-articulate
understanding of these conceptions, and that is true, but the
conceptions which underlie our practice are still in an important sense conceptions for us.

We can thus see two important areas of discourse, which at
least prima facie seem to be senseful and fruitful, and which
are foreclosed by the atomist-instrumentalist conception. The
first is that of common states—the spirit of a community, the
quality of common deliberation—which is embodied in a society's institutions and/or practices. The second is the vocabulary for the characterization of man and society which is implicit in these same institutions and practices.

What is the relation between these two? It is not that the
"vocabulary," that is, the conceptions implicit in our practices
determines uniquely our common states. Two societies with
the same institutions can have a quite different spirit or quality
of collective life; just as very different propositions can be
framed in the same vocabulary. But just as with vocabularies,
the underlying conceptions implicit in our institutions restrict
the range of what we can achieve as a common state. If we
live in a civilization that votes, we cannot hope to recapture
the kind of unity around a moving non-concatenating consensus which the traditional village had; or rather we achieve
this only in small, intimate communities—perhaps in certain
family relations.

But the institutional "vocabulary" provides more than the

limits to what we can aspire to. The underlying conceptions of man and society are not neutral descriptions. They offer conceptions of the proper or improper, the excellent and the deviant. There is not space to argue it here, but I would claim that neutral conceptions of man and society sufficiently rich to underlie social practice are an impossibility. In any case, we can readily see this in the above example. Voting as an institution with the point of concatenating social decision, posits certain norms which usually guide the detailed rules laid down in any voting procedure: the voter should be able to decide independently in full knowledge, the majority outcome prevails, and so on. More profoundly, the institution of voting is linked in our civilization with the aspiration to individual and group autonomy, to the ideal of self-determination, on so on.

Our institutional "vocabulary" also invites us to "say" certain things, to aspire to certain states. It is a misfortune in a civilization when there is a widespread alienation of sympathy from the ideals underlying important institutions, or where the ideals underlying different institutions enter into conflict. A society in this predicament may be pushed towards a fundamental change in its institutions and practices, but this is never easy and is often not possible, or only at horrendous cost.

But whatever one thinks of this latter affirmation, it is plain that a whole host of issues, concerning the quality of political life, the nature of political community, the underlying aspirations of a society, the limits to and conditions of change, the nature of the diversity between societies and over time—these and many other questions are open once we step outside the ambit of the dominant atomist-instrumentalist conception; while they remain closed, or can be raised only in a quite different, and I would argue, distorted form as long as one remains within it.

The issue between the instrumentalist conception and those who want to talk of common states is plainly an important one for the philosophy of science, of political science, in particular. The important factors and conditions of political life will be understood very differently from the different standpoints. Instrumentalists will try to understand and account for common states by correlating facts about institutions and facts about individuals' attitudes and actions. An example of this is the definition of "political culture" by Almond and Powell.

But it is plainly also an extremely important issue in our discourse about the political good. This is indeed the side from which we approached it above: the main reason why people want to talk about common states, in the sense we are using this expression here, is that they want to talk about the quality of common deliberation, or the quality of community life, or something of the sort. They are looking for a language in which to talk about the better and worse.

We can approach this issue, as it were, from these two directions. Why is it important to approach it from the first, to take it up as an issue in the philosophy of science? The obvious answer is that any language adequate as a language of the political good must also allow us to give a reasoned account of political society. And this is indeed the principle underlying our whole tradition of political theory. But beyond the fact that this principle is challenged today by those who want to distinguish explanation from evaluation, there is a particular view of science, widely held by those who support the atomist-instrumentalist conception, which would deny the title "science" to most of what has passed in the tradition of political theory as a reasoned account of the political. "Science" is to be restricted to accounts meeting certain standards of rigor and verification. Nor is this just a trivial issue of redefinition; the implication is that other forms of reasoned account—those we might find in Plato, Aristotle, Aquinas—are to be classed as "philosophical" or "metaphysical" in a pejorative sense, which is to say that they cannot be considered claims to knowledge in the same serious sense as the deliverances of "science."

This is a view of science which defines its boundaries by

epistemological criteria. The background reasoning concerns the conditions of valid, intersubjectively verifiable knowledge. One of the principal, if not the principal support for the instrumentalist conception stems from arguments which purport to show that it alone meets the epistemological conditions of science in the strong sense, that these are violated by rival conceptions that wish to give a place to common states or to talk about the implicit "vocabulary" of institutions. Of course, most people tend to accept the atomist-instrumentalist conception because it meets their experience: the experience of contemporary men in society who have formed an identity as individual agents, or in relation to some partial group, while looking on their political society as an environment in which their goals are attained or frustrated. We may judge that this fact of modern experience is the main reason for the popularity of the instrumentalist view. But when the protagonists of this conception argue for it in a theoretical context, the principal reason they adduce tends to be the epistemological one. This is one of the reasons why the debate between instrumentalists and their opponents is so much a dialogue of the deaf, as we shall see below. The debate is shot through with cross-purposes.

Now the epistemological tradition, which has been called empiricist, or latterly positivist, cannot accept this predicament as admissible in science. The principle is constantly emphasized that scientific results have to be "replicable," that everyone who puts himself in the position to make the relevant observations must come up with the same result. Faced with an interpretive dispute of the kind described in the last paragraph, one recourse would be to conclude that one or both of the disputants lacked the moral understanding or vision to see the point of the examples cited. But for the empiricist view this conclusion is quite inadmissible. It is a violation of the principle that results be replicable. We cannot claim as a valid ground for non-replication of a result that someone was lacking in understanding or vision. This is not what "replication" means in the empiricist tradition. The roots of this go back to the original empiricist theory of the basis of knowledge in "impressions" which impinge on the subject regardless of his degree of insight or understanding. But whatever its origins, the notion of replicability that takes no account of vision is basic to the current dominant theory of science.

If we accept this notion of replicability as a condition of scientific knowledge, then what we have called common states are excluded from the vocabulary of science. Or we can allow them only to the extent that we can find criteria for them in brute data, which in the end amounts to the same thing. For what are the candidates for brute data in the social sphere? The overt actions of individuals, insofar as the description of the action can be read without dispute off the overtly observable behavior of these individuals; the attitudes of individuals, insofar as these can be "operationalized" in brute data, for instance, in terms of responses to set questions; and also explicitly conventionalized institutional structures and events. The last play an important role in political science that follows the empiricist requirements. An explicitly conventionalized institutional event is, for instance, the casting of a vote. By explicit convention, certain definite movements, or markings or whatever are given the significance of a vote cast for some measure or party. Here there are reasons in social practice for making the issue whether this kind of event has taken place beyond interpretive dispute. It has to be clear, without regard to anyone's level of understanding or vision, how many electors have voted for each party at this polling station; our institutions require this to function. So a vote has to be related by convention to some brute-data-identifiable overt behavior. This kind of institutional event is thus tailor-made for an empiricist science of society.

What we have called common states have to be translated such that criteria can be give for them in brute data. Thus the spirit of a community, as we saw, is reinterpreted as the aggregate of individual attitudes, or the way in which some individual attitudes condition others. To study the conditions of different qualities of common life is to study how some attitudes repercuss on others, or institutions affect individual attitudes, or are affected by them; or their correlations with changes in other factors, such as economic growth, urbanization, level of education, and so on. But this means that common states have to be re-interpreted as concatenations of individual states, which is to say that they are not admitted at all. Hence the weight of the empiricist tradition tells in favor of the instrumentalist conception, the view that institutions are to be seen as instruments in relation to goals of individuals, independently defined. It reads common states out as inadmissible in scientific discourse. But this, as we saw above, is no trivial revision of a stipulative definition, a decision to reserve the word "science" to a study grounded in replicable data, while leaving other forms of reasoned discourse unchallenged. On the contrary, the epistemological assumptions of the empiricist tradition are that what lacks the appropriate data base cannot be an object of knowledge; so that on this view common states are not just ruled out of the language of a certain kind of science but are suspect altogether as objects of knowledge. Discourse about such things is "philosophical" in a pejorative sense, in the sense that it is not really knowledge.

We have, in other words, a modern tradition in philosophy of science in which epistemological considerations are made basic. Epistemology dictates ontology. Only those realities can be admitted for which criteria can be given in brute data. Common states cannot be grounded in this type of criterion, and therefore they cannot be admitted into reasoned discourse about politics.

This is why a contemporary study of politics or training in political theory has to address itself to issues in the philosophy of science. If a basic aim of this training, as I mentioned at the outset, is to make people multilingual philosophically about the polity; and if in our context, this means supplementing the language of the atomist-instrumentalist conception, which is the most readily and easily available, both intellectually and in experience, to most people in our civilization, with languages which allow for common states and the expressive dimension of institution and practices; then we have to address those epistemological prejudices that most effectively entrench uni-linguism, which most strongly tend to persuade us that only one language, that of the atomist–instrumentalist conception, makes sense.

So training in political thought should engage with the issues of the philosophy in science, and that on three levels. First, we have to address ourselves to what has been the main focus of the philosophy of science, the epistemological arguments and theories. We have to confront and examine the thesis that has become an inarticulate belief, one might say a prejudice, for many, that we can only speak of knowledge where we have replicable results, in the empiricist sense of "replicable." We have to examine whether we can speak of valid claims to knowledge in domains where interpretive disputes are ineradicable, where inadequacies of understanding or insight may make it impossible because of deep differences of moral vision. The issue here is of the nature of knowledge, and it spreads beyond the confines of political theory. The issues here have been discussed by philosophers who were not concerned with the impact of their thought on politics, as well as by some who were.

Second, we have to raise the issue of the place of epistemology in our reflection about politics. For the debate between instrumentalists and their opponents generally goes much deeper than a disagreement in epistemology. There is not even agreement that this is where the difference lies. Instrumentalists generally have been deeply influenced by the empiricist tradition, and have tended to claim that the crucial question is one of epistemology, and that the decisive grounds for their adopting the position they do are epistemological. But their opponents tend rather to hold that the real motivation for holding some fundamental position of political ontology must be one's experience of political reality and the kind of moral vision which grows from it. Thus from the outside, it appears much more plausible that instrumentalists are such because they have an experience of the polity as external, in the sense that it is not among those features of their world by which they define their identity, which will rather be some family or cultural or ethnic tradition, or perhaps some moral or ideological position. Instead, political institutions will be seen as external to these and as furthering or hindering the goals springing from their identifications or which they from time to time take on. Or instrumentalists are such because their experience as individual subjects in modern civilization makes the ideal of the self-defining subject who *ought to* be externally related to his political institutions as to instruments a plausible one. These two kinds of experience (which may of course go together) and others similar seem much more plausible as grounds for the instrumentalist position.

Not that these are to be seen as grounds which are *not* reasons, as having to be in the domain of irrational causation. On the contrary, those who stand outside the instrumentalist tradition are quite ready to discourse rationally about the nature of social experience, and the conceptions of man implicit in our institutions, practices, and in the common life of our society. And therefore they can quite well conceive a view of the human condition which is rationally grounded on properly reflected social experience, where one is aware of the way social experience has helped shape one's thought, and has through this awareness satisfied oneself that one's conception is well grounded. This is the claim made, for instance, by "critical" theories in the Marxist tradition, which claim to lay bare the way existing reality conditions our thought about the human condition and, precisely in laying this bare to transcend it.

Hence those who are critical of the atomist-instrumentalist view are wont to invite their opponents to discuss what they think are the really weighty reasons for adopting, e.g., an atomist view of the human social predicament. They cannot really believe that something so fragile and speculative, something so shakily grounded on uncertain analogies, as the epistemological requirements laid down by empiricism could *really* be the decisive grounds for adopting something as weighty as a social ontology. For them, epistemological arguments *are* the most decisive and weighty ones. As for social experience, the concepts we need to talk about this are not allowed into the charmed circle of scientific discourse, because they mostly deal with realities for which we cannot find criteria in brute data; hence arguments in these terms are without weight, and can be seen only as attempts to discredit their views by some attribution of disreputable social or ideological association.

Thus it is that the issue between instrumentalists and their colleagues is of that profound kind which makes it difficult to join the dispute, since there is not even a basic consensus as to what it is about, or how to go about resolving it. Consequently, the study of the philosophy of the science of society has to raise not only the issue about knowledge and its verification, but also the question of the place and relevance of this issue in our self-understanding. Can an epistemological view be itself criticized by tracing its motivations in social experience or moral aspiration? How can these two enquiries be related? This complex of questions ramifies very far and deep. It involves the questions of what is often called philosophical anthropology, questions about the nature of the human subject; and, beyond these, about the nature of society; and, beyond these in turn, about the historicity of human experience. The issue concerns the place of scientific enquiry in the experience of the human subject; for it is this which determines whether any purely epistemological arguments *can* be ultimate, or whether, on the contrary, the ultimate context of argument is rather the philosophy of history.

There is a third issue at stake here, in which once again the two sides are at cross purposes. I said above that the principal motivation for discussing such matters as the quality of common deliberation was to clarify questions about the political good. Those who do so proceed on the understanding that elaborating an adequate explanatory terminology and an adequate language to talk about the good go hand in hand, that these two languages are closely linked. But it is a central belief of the empiricist tradition that the context of explanation is quite independent of that of evaluation, and should be quite clearly distinguished. The roots of this view in empiricist thought are too complex to trace here, but one connection is evident. It is clear that any language which at once describes and evaluates is going to be inherently contestable, and open to the kind of unarbitrable interpretive disputes which thought by empiricists to be incompatible with scientific discourse. Consequently, empiricist theories have tended to make it a requirement of any adequate data language that it be "neutral." Discussion of the good, called in this language "evaluation," then intervenes as a reaction of the subject to the "facts," which are in themselves neutral.

The various theories about value freedom and the gap between facts and values are thus another bone of contention between instrumentalists and their opponents. They represent another disagreement about the very geography of the terrain in dispute, about the relevance of the issues to each other, about what constitutes a proof or a valid argument. For one side, no conclusions are valid to the good from the nature of things, or of the human social predicament; for the other, the only adequate explanatory language for man in society is one which also helps define what is good in the political realm.

There is therefore a third issue which has to be explored. It is again a very wide-ranging issue, which concerns the nature of "evaluation" and its place in human thought. But it involves raising again the question of the kind of discourse which can be a scientific discourse of society or the polity, and the relation this discourse has to that in which we reason about the good. It requires that we ask the question whether and in what way scientific enquiry must be "neutral" or "value free."

MARXISM AS
A POLITICAL PHILOSOPHY

MIHAILO MARKOVIĆ

It seems paradoxical that Marxism, which is more political than any other trend of contemporary philosophy, never systematically developed its political philosophy.

It is more political in two important senses: As a theory of revolution, it directly challenges the existing political structure of the capitalist world; where it is an official ideology of the bureaucratic élite, it is used as the justification of the existing political system.

There are several reasons why it was never systematically developed.

Marx himself resisted systematic development of philosophy. In his opinion, philosophy pure and speculative, isolated from concrete scientific inquiry, divorced from practice was passé. It was transcended within his critical social theory. But there it remained as the very foundation of any radical, critical humanist, *praxis*-oriented thinking. This implicit philosophical deep structure of "the critique of political economy" still lives as a rich, if poorly utilized, potential for any critical contemporary social thought.

It was Engels who formulated explicitly the view that traditional philosophical disciplines covering certain fields of reality, such as "philosophy of law," "philosophy of nature," "philosophy of history," "political philosophy," were merely the expression of a metaphysical tendency to speculate about the world where rigorous scientific study was already possible. What remained of all philosophy, in his opinion, was the study of laws of thought—formal logic and dialectic.

Although this analysis was never taken quite literally, the followers of Marx and Engels severely restricted the scope of philosophy. Lenin, for example, wrote only on epistemological and methodological issues. His writings on the theory of party, of the state, of the revolution were never considered philosophical. With Plekhanov, who coined the term "dialectical materialism," a demarcation line quite alien to the spirit of Marx's original thought developed: on the one hand, philosophy, reduced to the explanation of the materialist point of view and basic features of the dialectical method; on the other hand, historical materialism, as a substitute for general sociology, dealing in a quasi-empirical way with social structure and basic laws of social development.

The reduction of philosophy to the value-free study of knowledge went side by side with an essentially pragmatic treatment of politics. Marx rather underestimated politics by reducing it to a part of the social superstructure. Political power was hardly regarded by him as an independent objective determinant; it was rather a derivative of the relations of production. On the other hand, Marx considered politics a mere "sphere of alienation," the activity of forces estranged from human beings who created them. That is why he held that social revolution had not to be identified with political revolution, that the latter had "a narrow horizon" and led to the rule of an élite. That is why he was convinced that the state must be transcended by the "association of immediate producers," which would no longer be a purely political institution.

The subsequent history of Marxism in either its Social-Democratic or its Bolshevik form, is not compatible with all these basic assumptions. A "mere superstructure," politics became the most essential sphere of Marxist practical activity. Far from being a mere consequence of economic changes, politics sometimes became their cause. Political revolution in Marx's theory had to be only "an episode" of the global social revolution; the latter now was reduced to this episode. And the more a revolutionary became involved in daily political struggle for winning power, the more he risked becoming an alienated being himself.

The result is well known: Wherever political power was seized under the flag of Marxism it did not take much time before the development of original Marxian critical humanism—the only genuine theoretical basis for any revolutionary political thought—was condemned as subversive ("revisionist," "abstract-humanist," "neo-leftist," "anarcho-liberal," etc.). Political organizations and institutions that emerged on the basis of this new power structure retained Marxist rhetoric, but they had a vested interest in the preservation of a complete split between philosophy and politics: there, an abstract, impotent, harmless speculative thought; here, a purely pragmatic, ideological political practice.

However, it is possible to move in an altogether different direction. If *praxis* is the essential human characteristic; if consciousness is not only a reflection of reality but also its critique and a project of its qualitative change; if, consequently, all theory should be *praxis*-oriented, and all rational activity theory-laden, then political life cannot but become one of the important subjects of critical philosophical inquiry.

That does not imply that Marxist political philosophy should be treated as an isolated discipline, sharply delineated from other philosophical and scientific disciplines. It is one of the distinguishing characteristics of this philosophical tradition that it does not allow a narrow professional division of work and the fragmentation of its subject matter. This kind of theory deals with human historical reality as a concrete whole. All important social problems are multidimensional, the political dimension being only one among them. However, both theoretical enquiry and teaching process may focus on just this one dimension. It is essential only to be aware that, whatever may be gained by this analytical procedure, it is only one stage in the process of study, only a part of a totality.

Taking into account that the basic theoretical core of Marxist philosophy is constituted by a critical anthropology and that the whole theory is *praxis*-oriented, it follows that at least the following three components must constitute the structure of a properly interpreted Marxist political philosophy.

The first part deals with its theoretical and methodological foundations. Here begins the discussion of human nature, of basic human dispositions and needs, of the notion of *praxis* and self-realization, of the idea of alienation and universal human emancipation. Here also belongs the analysis of dialectical regulative principles of research in their application to political life.

The second part has to deal with the problems of the political philosophy proper: the nature of politics, the place of politics in the global structure of social life (its interrelations with technology, economy, law, culture), the purpose and the functions of the state, the nature of the political party, the separation of political powers, the centralist versus the decentralized state, the monolithic versus the pluralist state, the protection of minorities, individual political rights. As essentially a theory that tends to transcend class society, with its injustice and alienation, Marxist political philosophy will be a radical critique of both bourgeois and bureaucratic political institutions and practices.

The third part would be constituted by the analysis of the practical political implications of that critique. The practical form of human emancipation and of the transcendence of bourgeois and bureaucratic institutions is revolution. The crucial issues are here: the explication of the concept of social revolution and the determination within the global revolution of the place and importance of the seizure of political power. Related issues are the nature of the revolutionary movement, the strategy of violent versus non-violent revolutionary struggle, the interrelationships among different liberation movements (of oppressed classes, nations, races, women). The concluding subjects would be the future of politics, the transcendence of the state and the party as the forms of political organization, the political model of a future, self-governing society.

One of the most difficult and indeed crucial issues of a political philosophy is the justification of its value judgments. There always has been a tendency in philosophy to avoid value judgments altogether. If this could be done, political philosophy would be reduced to a mere analysis of concepts used in the language of politics and political theory. This preliminary work is necessary but is far from covering the whole field. But even this cannot be done, because any analysis of that kind imports tacitly some hidden initial value judgments. The proper questions for all those who are eager to secure some kind of objectivity of political philosophy are not how to avoid any value judgments, but how to bring them to the level of *critical* consciousness, how to reduce them to a *necessary minimum* from which all others could be derived, and how to ensure that these have a *universal* human character instead of merely expressing the vested interests of a particular social group.

Whatever other political philosophers might claim, Marxists have to admit that they make ample use of value judgments: They are implicit in every critical statement. But when the difficult question of justification arises, one hardly finds a satisfactory way of coping with it in the existing literature. There are two established ways of avoiding justification. One consists in formulating value judgments in the form of indicating (factual) statements. That is the way ideologues have always proceeded. The second way consists in pretending that the concept of possibility suffices to express whatever a critical theorist might wish to say. (For example, a "good" society would be one which does not yet exist but "is possible." Ideals would be construed simply as possibilities.) But this is clearly an illusion. In each situation there are many possibilities, and any human being who wants to contribute actively to molding his individual and social life must choose, must commit himself to the realization of one among these many possibilities. The choice is conditioned by some desire, need, or interest, and the problem is sometimes to bring these to consciousness. This analysis of actions in terms of *the possible* in fact tacitly presupposes the idea of the *optimal* possible.

Those Marxists who realize that here a non-factual, non-scientific dimension is present very often prefer the easiest way out. The whole vast field of goals, purposes, interests, values, needs, preferences is simply covered by one inarticulated idea: the mythological, the irrational, the utopian. The weakness of this approach is its complete absence of analysis and mediation. Irrational phenomena can be studied in rational ways. It is true that whatever is an external question with respect to a system can be relegated to the sphere of the irrational, mythological, utopian. However, an *external* question with reference to a poor, small-scale system may become an *internal* question with reference to a richer, broader larger-scale system that embraces the former as a special case. In such a way one can systematically remove the boundary between the rational and the irrational or the mythological until one reaches a very basic problem beyond which it seems that there is nowhere to go. Only there does one allow the very minimum of his value commitments to have axiomatic form.

More specifically, a possible Marxist procedure of justification in political philosophy would be as follows: a concrete individual decision (for example, to join a guerilla unit) becomes meaningful and valuable in terms of the goals and practical preferences of that guerilla movement, and those goals and preferences would be considered historically progressive or conservative from the point of view of universal human emancipation and self-realization. The latter two concepts presuppose a concept of human nature and this concept involves a very basic choice among different, even contradictory, general features of human behavior observed in the course of human history. While all other issues become in this context theoretical and rational, this basic choice is the very limit of our philosophical anthropology.

100

MIHAILO MARKOVIĆ

This is no longer a purely theoretical, but also a practical, issue: a practical commitment to struggle for the creation of such historical conditions as would encourage and reinforce manifestation of human characteristics selected by us as desirable ("positive"), while at the same time discouraging and blocking the manifestation of other undesirable ("negative") human features. There is nothing mythological or irrational about this. It is not the case that whatever cannot be demonstrated is irrational. We could even have good reasons to prefer one choice to the other. Similar choices have already been made in history: some by the wisest utopian thinkers and poets, some by the greatest criminals. Some past choices have invariably brought about periods of peace, prosperity, creativity, and cultural flowering; some have led to vast destruction and general decline.

Political philosophy does not start *ab ovo*. There are millennia of preceding political practice with all its variations and testing different institutions, forms of political organization, strategies of struggle. This vast experience is crystallized in the forms of alternative sets of principles. These principles constitute the *a priori* of each systematic political philosophy. But because these *a priori* principles have historical character, they must not be regarded as dogmas; they are revisable in light of subsequent experience; they are even testable. To affirm them amounts to saying that if certain specifiable favorable social conditions were to be created, certain desirable latent dispositions would be manifested by all human individuals, whereas undesirable, "negative" dispositions would tend to disappear. In this way, actual testing of alternative political philosophies is possible in principle. As a matter of fact, such testing takes place when a political philosophy becomes a guide to practical political life in a certain country under certain conditions. That is why comparative study of political systems could be of considerable help, provided that political philosophies get realized without enormous distortions (which, surely, is very often the case).

What distinguishes Marxist political thought methodologically from other traditions is not so much the way in which it *justifies* its concepts and propositions as the way in which it *generates* them and the direction in which it *develops* them. The basic purpose of political thought (in the tradition of Marx) is a critical analysis of a given reality. The specific dialectical features of this critical analysis are the following:

1. It is *radical*, in the sense that it starts from the root, and the root, *radex*, of all social phenomena is man. Therefore critique of political institutions and patterns of political life is ultimately the critique of the human condition, not of mere inefficiency, inconsistency, instability, or other instrumental features.

2. Dialectical critique is *holistic* and *systematic*: it is not a mere piecemeal analysis of some partial fragment of human condition, but a critique of the global situation in which human beings are crippled, degraded, and deprived of their humanity. It follows that the subjects of the study are systems, totalities, and not isolated parts; such an approach reveals the possibilities of *structural transformation* of the system, not only of its *modifications*.

3. Study of *synchronic*, structural relations must be supplemented by the study of *diachronic* historical relations. Critical consciousness of a political reality presupposes not only knowledge of its origin, but, even more, a vision of its future possibilities.

4. In the light of future possibilities, some structural properties of the studied system would turn out to be its essential inner limitations and impediments for further development. The crucial aim of the critical analysis is to establish how the system can be transcended, i.e., which of its political institutions must be abolished in order to change the system and lift it to a possible higher level.

Concepts that emerge in this kind of inquiry will be of three different kinds: in addition to descriptive, *neutral* ones, there will be some which refer to the limitations (*concepts-ne-*

MIHAILO MARKOVIĆ

gations) and some that refer to the optimal possibilities (*concepts-ideals*). Compare, for example, alienated labor-work-*praxis*, and state-government-self-government.

Dialectical clarification of concepts goes considerably beyond common analytical clarification. Making sharp dichotomic distinctions is only the first approximation in the process of conceptual inquiry; deeper analysis reveals mediating instances between opposites. As a result, either new mediating concepts will be introduced, or initial static concepts will be given a dynamic interpretation allowing the idea of movement from one pole to the other.

Another important aspect of the clarification of concepts takes place in the process of their practical application. To define a term by establishing its connotation and/or denotation is to indicate only the basic core of its meaning. In the process of application, an initially abstract, simple concept becomes rich and concrete. On the one hand, we become aware of the whole network of other concepts with which it is linked; on the other, we find a cluster of specific types and individual cases to which it is applicable. The movement of thought from the philosophical to the empirical, from theory toward practice, is at the same time a movement from the abstract toward the concrete. That is one of the reasons why Marxist political philosophy has to move from the foundations toward discussion of problems which, strictly speaking, are outside the customary range of philosophy. But what is, for example, the idea of *emancipation* without a discussion of the model of self-government? What is the idea of *human nature* or of generic being (*Gattungswesen*) without a detailed psychological, linguistic, anthropological analysis of basic human capacities?

But when we now ask the question which are the basic, *desirable*, universal human capacities (and this is the question) how do we choose the ground on which all our political thought and indeed all social theory rests? A very brief answer would be that they are the existing potential abilities of each

individual worth developing, encouraging, reinforcing—
faculties to cope with all kinds of unexpected new situations,
to think and solve problems, to introduce purposeful novel-
ties into one's already structured activity, to create and interpret extremely complex symbols, to cultivate one's senses and
enormously enrich one's sensory experience of the world, to
harmonize relationships with other individuals of a human
community, to develop a critical consciousness of one's own
past and present life.

In one word, there is an enormously rich and creative potential in each human individual. This potential is wasted, and
this waste, this discrepancy between actual crippled existence
and the whole wealth of potential capacities is concisely expressed by the notion of *alienation*. Another negative, critical
concept, considerably more specific is *reification*, i.e., reduction of human being to a lifeless, mindless object—to a thing.

There are three overlapping basic concepts that refer to the
absence or transcendence of alienation. The most general is
self-realization, which refers to an individual or collective
human subject who succeeds in manifesting its latent capacities, whatever they are. *Emancipation* lays emphasis on
negative and positive freedom: overcoming external and
internal barriers to self-realization. *Praxis* is the activity of a
non-alienated human being; this is the specifically human,
free, creative activity by which an individual objectifies his
best abilities and at the same time satisfies the needs of other
human individuals.

These anthropological concepts are now the ground for a
radical critique of existing forms of political life and political
institutions.

Political activity has the character of political *praxis* if it offers each individual an opportunity to participate in the social
decisionmaking, if it is essentially a conscious and rational
coordination of social processes, if it is guided by universal
human needs and interests and enlightened by other creative
intellectual activities such as philosophy, science, and the arts.

Under those conditions, politics is indeed extremely attractive and constitutes an end in itself. But in a class society, politics lacks any of these characteristics. All real power is concentrated in the hands of a few. Thus politics becomes a struggle for seizing and keeping power; it has relatively little to do with self-realization and the satisfaction of true human needs. In order to succeed, politics has no real need for philosophical wisdom, ethical values, scientific truth, and beauty; often the more ruthless, amoral, manipulative it is, the greater are its chances to win. It involves constant tension, wars and violent rebellions against oppression. *Homo politicus* is a split person, *political society* is a pseudo-community torn by conflict.

Conflict is the natural consequence of an unnatural and completely unjust distribution of wealth and power. It can be avoided only if citizens are kept in the state of political apathy and if their attention is diverted to some other objectives. For some time it seemed that capitalism had managed to solve the problem by provoking a widespread consumerist attitude and by developing an interest in unnecessarily long hours of work, compensated by increasing purchase power. But consumerism is too wasteful to last much longer. Reduction of the material production expansion rate, coupled with the continuing rapid growth of productivity of work, leads to very substantial reduction of working hours and gradual socialization of the means of production. These trends, in all probability, lead to growing demands for participatory democracy.

In this light it becomes possible to understand the classical Marxist critique of the state and the "withering away of the state" theory. Much misunderstanding was caused by the elliptic, if not confused, argumentation of some Marxists. In criticizing the state as *the* form of political organization. Marxists need not emphasize only its negative feature, nor should "withering away" be identified with a mere destruction. One of the two basic functions of the state is not controversial: In every society there must be a minimum of order and protection from criminal activities of certain individuals; in every society there must be a certain measure of coordination and direction of production, transportation, education. The essential limitation of the state is its oppressive nature. It uses a formidable apparatus of force of highly organized violence (the standing army, the political police, the courts) whenever the ruling state officials feel that their particular interests are jeopardized and that the existing unjust distribution of power is seriously challenged. The intolerable limitation of the state is its division of citizens into a minority of permanently ruling *subjects* and a vast majority condemned to the status of permanently ruled *objects* expected to be loyal, obedient, quiet, and cooperative when needed. In order to justify such a division, classical liberalism developed the theory of the natural aggressiveness, destructiveness, and selfishness of men; therefore the natural state was taken to be a state of permanent war which ended only with the social contract and the establishment of political society. The more we know about primitive societies, the more groundless this whole conception of human nature looks, even when it is interpreted as a hypothetical construction. In all likelihood, human aggressiveness is precisely the product of unfulfilled, repressed life in political society and its correlate, market-governed civil society.

The party as the unique form of political mass organization requires an analogous critique. Surprisingly, this is almost absent among Marxists. They debate the issue of inner party democracy and sometimes the issue of the multiparty political system versus one-party rule. However, in the light of the basic premises of Marx's political thought, a quite legitimate question is: Can a revolutionary movement achieve at all a profound social transformation if it led by a political organization that has the form of a party? This type of organization was generated in bourgeois society and preserves some distinctly bourgeois relationships and habits of political behavior. Its primary objective, to which everything else is subordinated, is to *seize and firmly keep political power*. Its structure is completely *hierarchical*, and its decision-making is even more authoritarian than in any bourgeois party. This may be inevitable in a persecuted, outlawed, clandestine organization, but it becomes a habit that survives after victory. There is an emphasis on strict *discipline*. At first it is internalized and allows a wide range of autonomous decision-making; in the conditions of "peaceful building up of socialism" it is redundant; it becomes external and quickly leads to heteronomy and duplicity of behavior. The theory of a party, the political consciousness of its members, is necessarily more or less *ideological*: As soon as the party develops its image as the indispensable vanguard of the revolutionary movement and fully identifies *the cause* with its own particular interest, its perception of reality becomes systematically biased and frozen, and its struggle against heretics intensifies. The propaganda effort of the party will inevitably involve an element of *manipulation*: Masses need faith and faith must be orthodox.

The issue here is not whether any political organization is needed. Many functions performed by the parties must survive in any modern society, such as articulation of different social needs in the form of practical programs, political education, control of the executive power and criticism of the weaknesses of implemented policy, taking positions in existing social conflicts, and finding ways of resolving these conflicts. These functions could be performed by all kinds of political organizations (leagues, clubs, unions) lacking the defining characteristics of the parties. This means, furthermore, that a revolutionary movement must not be merely political. Its decision-making should be as decentralized as possible; the leadership must rotate and should be as much exposed to criticism from the rank-and-file as conditions allow. The common will of the movement could be created by agreeing on a small number of basic goals. (When there is an objectively revolutionary situation, sectarian ideological disputes become irrelevant.) Spreading political information would require maximum honesty. The long-range effect of manipulation is loss of credibility, and a movement that struggles for a far-reaching social transformation, not merely for the seizure of power, must be future-oriented and preserve credibility.

This leads us to the problem of revolution. By now it must have become quite clear that the defining characteristics of a revolution in Marx's sense are neither use of violence, nor overthrow of a government and seizure of political power, nor even the economic collapse of the system. Marx himself spoke of a possible peaceful social revolution in England, the Netherlands, and America. He made it quite clear that the overthrow of bourgeois political power would be only its introductory stage. That economic collapse is far from being a necessary condition of revolution follows from Marx's description of the economic measures of the transition period in the *Communist Manifesto*. These measures are indeed very cautious and gradual, intended to preserve the continuity of economic functioning.

A Marxian notion of revolution can be properly understood only when one grasps the general *dialectical* idea of *transcendence (Aufhebung)*. A given social system (socioeconomic formation) has certain structural characteristics that arrest further development and prevent the realization of already existing historical possibilities of the given society. For example, private property and commodity production regulated by the market involve a tremendous waste, preventing at the same time the satisfaction of many basic needs; the existence of the state prevents a democratic rational coordination with the maximum participation of each citizen. A revolution is essentially the transcendence of these inner limitations—and it is irrelevant whether physical violence is used (preferably not), or whether change takes place in one discontinuous cataclysmic act or by a series of definitely directed gradual modifications.

One of the important practical implications of such a redefinition of revolution is the rehabilitation of the strategy of non-violent social change. Marxist literature on this subject is almost nonexistent, although it becomes increasingly clear that most revolutions in advanced industrial countries will take place—and are already taking place—precisely in a more or less non-violent form. Institutions undergo a steady gradual transformation. Capitalism already has begun to disappear under the very eyes of those who wait for the revolution, or who see it completed where it has only started and got blocked. For Schumpeter, a few decades ago, capitalists were only owners without the function of management. If, in coming years, a government (for example, a Labour government in Great Britain) decides that these owners get only a fixed interest and no more variable share of profit, they will socially stop being capitalists, although they will remain more or less rich people (who exist in present day socialism and will survive in future society). What still essentially differentiates a Marxist from a Gandhian or a Quaker is that he does not commit himself unconditionally and unhistorically to either a violent or a non-violent strategy of revolutionary struggle. From a number of important characteristics of a historical situation (especially the strength of a center of power, the degree of its mass support, the amount of structural violence already existing in society, willingness of the ruling class to make concessions and allow necessary reforms) would depend which of the two strategies would be preferable.

The political structure of the new society may be characterized as self-government. The idea stems from utopian and anarchist thinkers, but it also follows from Marx's humanist philosophy and is explicitly present in both his early and his mature works.[1] In order to build up a theoretical model of self-government, one has to take into account not only Marx's basic ideas but also democratic and socialist achievements within contemporary advanced capitalist countries, and especially the experiences of Yugoslavia, where initial forms of self-government were introduced a quarter-century ago. I can here only outline, in the most concise possible way, the main features of the model.

The basic assumption of the model is the transcendence of any monopoly of economic and political power, whether in the hands of a bourgeoisie, or of a political bureaucracy or technocracy. A network of workers' councils, assemblies, and other organs of self-government at all levels of social organization would assume responsibility for *basic* decision-making. *Technical* dimensions of decision-making would naturally remain in the hands of experts, managers, competent administrators. It is essential, however, that the technical management be fully subordinated to the organs of self-government. Daily technical operation of the former would depend on the policy decisions of the latter. It is also essential not to identify self-government with a poorly coordinated *decentralized* system. In addition to councils at the social *micro-level* (in working organizations and living communities), there must also be organs of self-government at the *macro-level* (for the whole branches of activity and regions, eventually central assemblies for the global society).

What distinguishes any member of an organ of self-government from a professional politician, a state bureaucrat, is that the former has been democratically elected for a limited period of time, obliged to account regularly to his electorate for the way he represents them, ready to resign or to be recalled if he disagrees with the views and desires of the electorate. Most important of all, his function offers responsibility and honor, but not material privileges—a concealed form of exploitation, which is precisely the economic ground of the new "socialist," non-Weberian bureaucracy.

One of the most difficult problems that a system of self-government has to solve is how to secure a necessary measure of efficiency and rational direction by building up a central political authority and at the same time prevent undesirable concentration of political power in a few hands.

Powers must obviously be separated. Each democratic revolution must come up with a new idea of separation of powers. A society in which central political institutions bear responsibility not only for legislative, executive, and judicial functions but for all socially necessary work, education, and social security, the social decision-making will include some new dimensions, especially planning, overall control, and cadres policy. These powers would be divided among separate councils within a central assembly of self-government.

There is a tremendous confusion among Marxists concerning the centralization–decentralization issue. Authoritarian bureaucratic planning and control of all social life versus decentralization and dismantling of all planning is a misconceived dilemma. The trouble with bureaucratic decision-making is not that it is central, but that it is *alienated* and *authoritarian*. Being central in this case does not involve being efficient. Different social functions require different degrees of centralization. Optimal energy and transportation policies, for example, require considerable centralization. Culture does not. Different societies at different levels of development could distribute responsibilities among different levels of self-government in a more centralized or more decentralized way.

It is essential, however, that all power be delegated by the organs of *direct democracy*. The basic organs of self-government in enterprises and communes have to decide how much power, and for which type of tasks, they wish to transfer to the higher-level organs in the interest of better coordination and more rational direction. At any moment they must be able to challenge this rationality or to increase the level of decentralization.

Marxists have not paid enough attention to the problem of protection of the rights of minorities. The introduction of the principle of "democratic centralism" as the crucial principle of the party organization obliging the minority merely to conform to the majority created the impression that Marxism indeed *necessarily* involved some sort of totalitarianism. This does not follow: A revolutionary movement need not have the form of a party, and even the party need not follow the principle of "democratic centralism" without any qualification. (Lenin's type of the Communist party is in fact characteristic for backward countries.) The way Marxists sometimes treat the problem of national minorities (in Lenin's theory and in present-day Yugoslav practice) gives important hints as to how the problem could be solved in its most general form.

When a kind of particular interest is very important from the point of view of the unity of society, then, on certain vital issues, either a *veto power* will be at the disposal of a minority; or an equal number of votes will be given to each group, no matter how big; or the issue will be decided not by vote but by *agreement*, involving negotiation and necessary compromises on all parts. When none of these rules is applicable, a minority outvoted on an important issue and convinced that the decision was wrong must be able to revive the issue as soon as attempts to implement the decision of the majority furnish new arguments against it.

Within the scope of a paper it has not been possible either to engage sufficiently in confrontation with other, non-Marxist political philosophies or to offer a developed critical analysis of various, alternative interpretations of Marxism. What I have tried to do has been to show how a systematic political philosophy based on Marx's humanist ideas and on some promising attempts of the implementation of "democratic socialism" might look in broad outline. If anyone objects that this is not Marxism, my reply will be: Strictly speaking, an orthodox Marxism is not possible. A theory based on the philosophy of *praxis* cannot be a mere replica, or commentary, or a mere exercise in the application of some ready-made dogmatically fixed principles. One can only choose a possible interpretation of the fundamental ideas which are still very much alive. One must fill the gaps, extrapolate, and generalize new practical experiences, project new possibilities. That is what Marx himself would have done had he been alive today.

1. For example, in his "Critique of Hegel's Doctrine of the State," Marx says that "human emancipation will be achieved only when man ceases to separate from himself his *forces propres* as a social power in the form of political power." In *The Poverty of Philosophy*, Marx declared that in the process of its development, the working class will replace the old civil society with an association which excludes classes and their contradictions. "Then there will no longer

THE STUDY OF TEXTS

ALLAN BLOOM

Our general theme is "How ought the next generation of political philosophers to be educated?" I suppose what is meant is really "How ought the next generation of professors of political philosophy to be educated?" We cannot prescribe to genius; and it can, for the most part, take care of itself. Philosophy is not a profession like medicine or shoemaking. Professors of political philosophy can, however, be trained, and their function is to take advantage of genius and to help to make it accessible to others. They can also help the philosophers by preserving in the form of a tradition what was taught by the philosophers—thereby both serving the public good and keeping alive the matter on which potential philosophers must feed.

But our question is a good one, for it contains an "ought"; and if we succeed in answering it, we shall prove that political philosophy is possible, that it is capable of producing "valid normative statements." Our claim to recognition stands or falls with this capacity. The question is also good because it forces us to take stock of ourselves from the most advantageous standpoint: our students. We cannot, from this perspective, fail to look beyond our specialties to the whole human being we should like to see come to be; and we must look to the most general problems of our discipline. No time could be more appropriate for our questioning, for political philosophy's claim to be the queen of the social sciences or the study of man as well as the guide of statesmen is scarcely honored. Political philosophy is in crisis; its very possibility is doubted, nay denied, by the most powerful movements of contemporary thought. And that crisis is identical with the crisis of the West, because the crisis of the West is a crisis of belief—belief in the justice of our principles.

In order to educate for political philosophy, there must be some agreement about what it is. It might be suggested that political philosophy is the quest for knowledge of the best way of life, of the most comprehensive good, or of justice and the best regime. This implies that there exists a good which is knowable. Both the existence of the good and our capacity to know it by reason are denied by positivism and historicism, the two most powerful intellectual forces of our time. One important strand of contemporary thought denies even the desirability of such knowledge.

Of course, political philosophy is the quest for such knowledge, not necessarily, nor even probably, its actualization. In fact, since philosophy, by its very name, implies the pursuit of wisdom—an unending search in which every certitude is counterpoised by a more powerful doubt—the best political philosophy can provide is clarity about the fundamental alternatives to the solution of the human problem. Here again there is a presupposition: there are permanent alternatives which can be identified.

Given that what is wanted is an openness to the fundamental alternatives, what education conduces most to it? I shall note only in passing the kind of character required for profiting from an education in political philosophy. Its presence must be assumed; one can at best encourage it; it cannot be made. The prime constituents are love of justice and love of truth. These two are in some measure in contradiction, and a discrete mating of the two is rare; for love of justice borders on and usually involves indignation, which overwhelms the dispassionateness and lack of partisanship requisite to science, while love of truth removes a man from that concern for the particular demanded by justice. Aristotle says that political science lies somewhere between mathematics and rhetoric. The attempt to make it mathematical would destroy its phenomena. Abandoning it to mere taste would be a renunciation of reason in the most important questions. It partakes of theory and practice, reason and passion, and from the two extreme perspectives seems either unscientific or not engaged. It is therefore particularly vulnerable to the temptations of the extremes—to sham science or fanatic commitment. (In this light the wildly varying dispositions toward political philosophy in the last generation can be seen as a particular expression of a perennial problem—a problem exacerbated by a new kind of science and a new kind of religiosity.) The man who practices political philosophy must make that union, impossible according to Pascal, between *l'esprit de géométrie* and *l'esprit de finesse*, and will appear open to the charges of being unscientific and irrelevant. He must resist public opinion and his own conscience.

Now, given this disposition, what is necessary for nourishing it properly? The answer is the careful study of texts, of the classic texts of the tradition—that and not much else. This is what is most needful—always, and particularly in our time. This assertion appeals neither to the behavioral scientists nor to those who think our purpose is not to understand reality but to change it. It seems at best merely scholarly, denying as it does the decisive superiority of our current knowledge over that of the past and the peculiarity or essentially unique character of our problems. These objections to the study of texts are perpetually made, and political philosophy by very definition both calls them forth and rejects them. But they appear particularly strong today, when knowledge of the tradition is particularly weak. Therefore they must be addressed.

First, to speak to the reasons for the concentration on texts at all times, as opposed to our very special need, it is hard to imagine serious reflection which begins *de novo*, which is not sublimated to a higher level by a richly developed literary-philosophic tradition, transmitted in the form of writings. However radical a break from the tradition a thinker may make, the consciousness of the problems, the very awareness that there are problems as well as the knowledge of what it takes to respond to them, comes from being imbued with that tradition. This is not to deny that the problems are permanent and ubiquitous or that the human mind is at all times and places potentially capable of grasping them. It is not an assertion that the character of knowledge is essentially traditional or that the mind is essentially related to a particular culture. But there are preconditions to the mind's activity; it must above all have substance on which to work. Raw experience does not suffice. Experience comes to sight in the form of opinion, and the examination and elaboration of opinions makes the experience broader and deeper. Only he who has seen through the eyes of profound and subtle observers can be aware of the complex articulation of things. Socrates without the teachings of Parmenides and Heraclitus would not have had his issues to address, nor would his superiority have been tested were his competition not of this quality. I venture to suggest that great philosophic men were almost always great scholars. They were studiers of their predecessors, not for the reasons which ordinarily motivate scholars, but because they believed, almost literally, that their salvation depended on it, that those earlier thinkers may have possessed the most important truths.

Now, great natural scientists have not in general needed to be great scholars. At most they have had to address themselves to the preceding generation of scientists in addition to their contemporaries. The modern natural sciences have been progressive, and their great success has made them a model for all learning. Their example would seem to prove that certain important questions can be decided forever, and that the thought of those who lived before their solution is decisively inferior to that of those who lived after.

Aristotle's knowledge of the movements of the heavens is doubtless inferior to that of almost any college student. The model of the natural sciences has contributed much to the contempt for tradition in philosophy. Scholarship would seem to belong to the same order of rank in relation to philosophy as does history of science in relation to science. History

of science is evidently of lower rank than science and is also
not necessary to it.

The issue is whether modern science is not a special off-
shoot of modern philosophy—which is surely questionable.
Its success may very well be due to its very partialness. The
doubts now current about both the goodness of natural science and its relation to the real world give some support to
this view. But, without entering into these difficult and
troubling questions, surely natural science is not the privi-
leged model. From the perspective of the whole, Aristotle
does not come off so badly. A scientist like Bertrand Russell
may despise him, but a philosopher like Hegel can show that,
in the most important respects, Aristotle is superior to New-
ton. And to do so, Hegel had to know Aristotle very well. If
Hegel had stayed within the confines of the scientific opinions
of his contemporaries, he would not have seen the great difficulties in them. Aristotle was the pre-condition of Hegel's
liberation. Machiavelli, Rousseau, and Nietzsche would not
have enjoyed their admirable intellectual freedom if they did
not know Plato well and had accepted the prevailing notion
that he had simply been refuted or outdated. Every new
beginning—like that of Descartes, for example—implies a
certain rejection of the past. But it takes on its significance in
the light of what it rejects. The new beginning becomes a tradition in its turn, and those who follow it forget its origins in
a confrontation with another kind of thought. They are tradi-
tion-bound, and when the new tradition proves to have difficulties of its own, they are no longer aware of an alternative to
it. Their perspective seems natural and, although itself problematic, superior to what went before, which is only known
in the light of their tradition.

If we do not have completed, final wisdom, then our most
important task is the articulation of the fundamental alternatives. This can be achieved only by maintaining an authentic
knowledge of the best earlier thought, understood in its own
terms, divested of distortions imparted to it by the thought
which superseded it. Descartes gave a full presentation not

only of the pre-scientific world but also of the previous philosophic interpretations of it. Those who followed him accepted his rejection of earlier thought without themselves having gone through his analysis. What was still a serious alternative for Descartes no longer was one to his followers, and knowledge of it decayed. Thus, knowledge of the tradition of philosophy is necessary to philosophy and required for philosophic freedom from tradition. Philosophy has, at its peaks, largely been dialogue between the greats, no matter how far separated in time. Without the voices which come from outside the cave constituted by our narrow horizon, we are ever more bound to it. And, according to at least one version, philosophy *is* liberation from the bonds which attach us to the cave.

In our time the study of texts is particularly needful. Never has the challenge to political philosophy been so great. Historicism, cultural relativism, and positivism join in agreeing that the old notions about the good and the way of knowing it must be wrong, that traditional political philosophy was a dream because it did not possess the historical insight or the awareness of the arbitrariness of value judgments. Although in doubt about most things, the modern movements are sure about that. They have not succeeded in finding a substitute guide for human life, and the present situation borders on nihilism. It behooves us to reflect on that situation, and to determine whether the understanding of things which results in it is adequate. The issue is whether our thought is derivative from a particular way of posing the problems, or whether it establishes its principles independently.

For example, the fact-value distinction is taken as a given by almost everyone today, no matter whether they are behavioral scientists or committed revolutionaries. Whether it has been proven that values cannot be derived from facts, or whether that very distinction has any grounding in the phenomena—as opposed to being a mere fiction resulting from certain doubtful philosophic interpretations of phenomena—

is hardly discussed. The distinction is removed from the context from which it was derived and treated as an independent truth. And the knowledge of that context and what is opposed to it has decayed.

The search for a fresh start would require a purging of acquired prejudices and of all the categories of thought and speech derived from contemporary or recent philosophy. This task requires a return to the beginning points of thought, to the pre-scientific or pre-philosophic or natural world. Otherwise one sees the world through the screen of one articulation of the phenomena or another and is locked into the interpretation which one wishes to question. And the origins are peculiarly difficult of access for us who live in a world transformed by science and an intellectual atmosphere permeated by ideology. Ours is the age when philosophy and science—i.e., a certain kind of philosophy and science—have triumphed.

Philosophy and science have become involved in life and have changed the world. They are no longer observers or monitors. This is a unique circumstance; in the past, science did not try to replace the errors of the cave by substituting itself for them. In doing so, it risked becoming itself an error and no longer having the means to correct itself. Previously, the world had a diversity not caused by science, from which science could gather its interpretations; now the world tends to become the result of a particular interpretation, and, thus, to bear witness to it. For example, an economist's hypothesis that man's primary motive is gain can now become policy: a nation which encouraged that motive might end up producing men who prove the hypothesis. Only by looking outside that nation would one be able to regain a basis for recovering man as he is and for calling the hypothesis into question. In general, our world and our minds have much in common with my example. There is a unanimity in the world about the principles of science, while we are approaching one about the principles of politics. To see the latter uniformity, one need only compare the serious intellectual alternatives advanced in the 1930s—alternatives already relatively impoverished, compared with the past—with those available today. Now there are practically nothing but liberals and communists, who also share much with respect to ends, and there are practically no regimes with any vitality which are not supported by one of these two kinds of thought. The principle of equality, which is surely not simply self-evident, and should be the result of enlightenment and should be able to be defended against its serious opponents, has degenerated into a prejudice. Now, most serious of all, we are losing competence not only in those authors who could challenge our favorite beliefs but also in those who could best support them. The self-awareness of modern man depends on a knowledge of our intellectual roots and on a quest to rediscover the world on which the artificial world created by modernity is more or less well-grounded.

The threatened character of our self-awareness is strikingly illustrated by the most celebrated book on questions of political thought published in the Anglo-Saxon world in recent years, John Rawls's *A Theory of Justice*. It presents a new theoretical ground for liberal democracy. But it begins by dismissing discussion of its egalitarian premise. It is only an analysis of what an egalitarian society should be, if you accept that equality is just. Rawls begins by assuming, or taking for granted, that which political philosophy always took as its task to prove or investigate. We can no longer take the alternatives seriously; we intuit the justice of equality. Thus the longing to *know* the truth about these questions is dogmatically denied its fulfillment and we are given over to what may only be the dominant prejudice of the day. Rawls devotes no time to proving that such knowledge is not accessible. From the outset the most important question, the one which motivated philosophy and the possible answer to which inspired and elevated those who think, is ruled out of bounds. But this is not what is most striking; it is rather Rawls's easygoingness about our situation, the absence of anguish over our impotence, the conviction that the consequences are not dreadful.

The other salient quality of this book, related to the first one, is the great ignorance of the tradition of political philosophy manifested in it. Although Rawls uses ideas which come to him through the tradition, they are accepted traditionally, used partially to support his predetermined purposes, and very frequently distorted. There is no indication that at any point he felt compelled to question his own framework because of the force of what came from outside.

Rawls's book attempts to renew the contract teaching of the state of nature theorists. But he abandons their insistence on nature and therefore finds himself without a sanction for justice and observance of the contract. More scholarship would have given him at least the outline of what would have been required to construct a meaningful contract. He would also have seen what possibilities have to be sacrificed in a contract teaching as opposed to one which e.g., regards man as naturally a political animal; and he would have been forced to come to grips with problems he hardly knows exist.

For example, Rawls puts forward a doctrine of "primary goods," ultimately derived from Hobbes. These "primary goods" are, in essence, means to any possible end, and are therefore good because desirable to all men, no matter what their end. Rawls says that money is one of the most important, if not the most important, of such goods. He does not realize that the maximization of wealth can only be considered unproblematically good if poverty is held to be a good by no one. But Christianity praised poverty; and Hobbes, who was quite aware of what he was doing, had to denigrate Christianity. His state-of-nature teaching is a substitute for the Biblical account of man's original situation. One has to decide between these two positions before an instrumental good can be considered simply good. Rawls really assumes that certain kinds of ends, for which the primary goods are evils, either do not exist or are untrue. He thus fails to present the radicalness of the political problem, which stems from the radical diversity of possible ends. He contributes to a narrowing of our horizons and an unfounded hopefulness about potential agreement among men. He accepts as a given Hobbes's transformation of religion or the world in which religion lives, and thereby reasons from a world that is unproblematic for him because, living in Hobbes's world, he no longer sees its problems. He is enabled to criticize Locke and Rousseau for intolerance when they proscribe certain religious beliefs from civil society because he sees that the religions can, contrary to Locke and Rousseau, live together in peace. What he does not see is that the religions he observes have been transformed by the Enlightenment thinkers and are only tame species of the genus religion. He utterly misses what Hobbes and Locke and Rousseau were doing. Religion is not a serious question to him. It is just another one of the many ends that can be pursued in a liberal society. He is unaware that liberal society is predicated on a certain understanding of religion, one that excludes other understandings. What is perhaps the most serious question facing a serious man—the religious question—is almost a matter of indifference to him.

I chose these two related matters of wealth and religion in Rawls because there is today a large measure of complacent agreement about them which needs most rigorous examination and doubt. The philosopher now, instead of waking us up, contributes to our sleep. Rawls is drawn completely into the circle of current opinion because he is closed to what is outside of it. He can say that universalization is not of the essence of Kant's moral teaching, showing that he has not reflected on what freedom is in Kant; he can call Nietzsche—perhaps the most extreme antiteleologist who ever lived, the man who called Darwin a teleologist—a teleologist; he can invoke Aristotle to support his view that the greatest possible complexity is desirable by referring to a passage where Aristotle says simplicity is best. If this were to be the type of nourishment provided by philosophy, our children would ing. That difference or change in taste can point the way to fundamental problems, such as the different value once set on moderation even by the apparently immoderate Machiavelli and Rousseau. This procedure results in a relatively small number of classic books, a list established not subjectively by means of current criteria, but generated immanently by the writers themselves. I argue that there is a high degree of agreement among the writers themselves as to who merits serious consideration. The men of quality know the men of quality. Moreover, from this internal dialogue between the books emerges a high degree of agreement about the permanent questions as opposed to the questions of the day.

The closest reading of these books is my prescription. But there is so much that stands in the way of such a close reading, at least as the core of an education. To begin with, to follow Tocqueville's analysis of American intellectual proclivities, we are not a theoretical people. The appearance of uselessness goes counter to our concentration on utility. The notion of speculation for the sake of speculation is not one that accords with any inner experience of the dominant part of the regime, and seems even to contain an element of immorality, particularly in things political which touch the passions so closely. In political science over the past thirty years, there have been two trends in regard to political philosophy, trends apparently contradictory, but issuing from the same source. Either political philosophy has been rejected as ineffective, or it has been embraced as the source of commitment to revolutionary change as opposed to the conformist tendencies of political science as a whole. Men like Pascal, who thought the only thing that counted was the unremitting quest for the knowledge of God, are not native to our soil. Nor are men like Archimedes, who destroyed all of his writings on his extraordinary inventions in engineering because they smacked of low necessity. We believe our business is too pressing for such self-indulgence. *Relevance* was just another expression of our deepest instinct. And connected with this untheoretical nature is a distrust or contempt for tradition. As Tocqueville puts it, tradition has no authoritative status for us. It is just another piece of information. Authority is no doubt contrary to the philosophic spirit, but respect for tradition helps to keep alive and give respect to what would not otherwise be taken seriously. The scholastics took Aristotle as an authority, which was surely a mistake. But thereby he was preserved and available for those capable of understanding. We, on the other hand, free from the prejudice in favor of old authority, are likely to neglect what it can teach us. The democratic principle tends to make every man the judge of what is worthwhile, and the authority of special intelligence is not more likely to be respected than that of wealth or birth, particularly inasmuch as it is less easy to recognize. There is an ever-diminishing impact of the books which gave men a common vision and a common spiritual substance. Families are no longer tied together by the Bible or Shakespeare or anything at all coming directly from books. These fundamental books caused a popular respect for books in general and provided a common universe of discourse, one linking the thinking part of the community with the rest of it. I have the habit of asking the students in my classes what books have moved them and permanently affected their lives. The answer usually, and more universally each year, is none. This is not a reading generation; reading is not the activity of leisure, and books are not where students expect to learn about how to live their lives. This is merely a culmination of the penchants Tocqueville so powerfully described. And the control on these penchants exercised by our intellectual tutelage to Europe, where philosophy and the literary tradition connected with it played a greater role and were more part of the real life of nations, has almost disappeared with our emancipation from them and the assimilation of their regimes and education to ours.

Our students, in addition to not loving books, possess two contrary dispositions which combine to undermine the study of books in the quest for truth. They are persuaded that values are relative, partly on intellectual grounds, partly because

such a belief seems more conducive to democracy and toler-
ance. Thus they know beforehand that the books are wrong
in their claim to decide questions of good and bad. At the
same time, they in general share an unquestioned and unquestionable—almost religious—conviction of the truth of the
principle of equality. Since this is a contentious issue in the
tradition, with many of the older writers against it, such
writers seem to be teachers of vice rather than thoughtful
men.

Once having overcome the prejudice against books, one is
still only at the beginning of the task of a fresh look at them.
Aside from the wide acceptance of historicism and positivism,
which makes the claims of the older writers seem deluded,
there are special doctrines which act as a screen between us
and the books and give us the impression that we know what
is most important about them before we begin reading them.
The common view that economic or psychological or historical factors determine the thought of philosophers of course
assumes that the philosophers are wrong, both because they
all argue that thought can be free from any other determination than the truth, and because one must know that an opinion is untrue to explain its source in anything other than the
truth. The sociology of knowledge is a misnomer; it can only
properly be called the sociology of error. And if it is true that
the philosophers are necessarily in error, then their study is
the business of triflers. That it is important to know that Plato
was an aristocrat or Hobbes a bourgeois, that Machiavelli was
a man of the Renaissance and Montesquieu a man of the Enlightenment, that Rousseau and Nietzsche were mad, seems
so self-evident that it is almost impossible to see how one
would proceed without such crutches. But as soon as one has
accepted these commonplaces, one has subverted the study of
the books, because such views teach us what to look for and
take as facts what needs to be proved. They also presuppose
that they emerge from a true framework, or one that is
metaphysically neutral, that the practitioners of this
scholarship cannot be subjected to a similar analysis. Almost

all modern scholarship, beginning with classical philology, started from the assumption that its fundamental ideas were superior to those of the authors it studied and placed these authors in a context alien to them. Even such simple categories as idealist and realist, liberal and conservative, are profoundly misleading although they seem to us as natural as night and day.

The only way to break out of this circle of subjectivism— and subjectivism it is, because, although arguing that it is objective, its adherents also admit somehow that they too are historically determined, and therefore tacitly accept that the next generation will interpret differently, making the philosophers nothing but the contradictory things various ages of scholars say about them—is to try to understand the philosophers as they understood themselves, to try to determine their intention, accepting the possibility that they may have fulfilled their intention and attained the truth. This is a naïve undertaking, but the recovery of innocence can be salutary. It implies a severe rupture, not only with the presuppositions of modern scholarship, but also with its results. One can be heartened by the reflection that Thomas Aquinas was a very good interpreter of Aristotle, and Rousseau of Plato, without the enormous apparatus that now stands between us and the texts.

What does it mean to understand the authors as they understood themselves? For example, Machiavelli says that he was doing something totally new. This claim is not generally accepted. More and more he is assimilated, on the one hand, to earlier thinkers, and on the other, to the more conventional thought of his own time. As I just mentioned, he is called a man of the Renaissance. But if Renaissance means anything, it means the rebirth of classical Greek and Roman antiquity. Machiavelli, however, rejected both the thought and the practice of classical antiquity. He believed he had found a new and superior ground on which to erect the structure of politics. In adopting the myth of the man of the Renaissance, one assumes what one cannot know—what the Renaissance was really like, and whether there was a typical man and thinker—and distorts with this imaginary standard what we can know—Machiavelli's text. We note the similarities between Machiavelli and his contemporaries, and become blind to the differences separating them. This provides a second general maxim: In what appears similar, one should look for the differences; and in the different, the similar; but particularly it is the differences on which one must concentrate. It is taken for granted that when Machiavelli adopts the language or the tone of his contemporaries that he does so fully and sincerely, but that when he argues for his peculiarity he is mistaken and vain. It is true that *The Prince* resembles the traditional mirrors of princes in some respects. But nothing in them resembles the teachings of e.g., *Prince* XV and XXV. Thrasymachus, to take another familiar comparison, surely agrees with Machiavelli that men pursue their private interest exclusively; he is "hard-headed," but he never suggests that this self-interest can be the basis of a policy conducive to the public interest.

All of these appealing generalizations are nothing but impediments. One should pick up *The Prince* and read it as though it were written by a contemporary, as though it were a personal communication to one about something of common concern. In this way we abandon the categories which we allow to become habitual due to a lack of a sense of urgency. A line-by-line, word-by-word analysis must be undertaken, for Machiavelli is a difficult writer, and we do not have the habit of reading carefully. The hardest thing of all is the simplest to formulate: Every word must be understood. It is hard because the eye tends to skip over just those things which are most shocking or most call into question our way of looking at things. One simple definition of the philosopher is that he is the man who thinks concretely without the aid of abstractions which order things but at the same time really hide them. The study of great philosophers is an education in concrete consciousness, but it can easily degenerate into a support for abstractions. This is the reason the novelist and

and tries to wonder. Our failure to see is a result not only of laziness or lack of intelligence but of our unwillingness to believe that Machiavelli could have thought or taught this or that thing. This unwillingness is a result either of our moralism or of certain notions about what men in the Renaissance thought. How often I have heard men of high intelligence, good will, and learning reject an obvious point, clearly stated in the text, with the remark, "No man in the sixteenth century could have thought such a thing!" To take another example, in the study of Plato, it is practically taken for granted that Socrates's trial was politically motivated and that the charge of impiety was only a pretext. This interpretation goes counter to everything the texts of the *Apology* and other dialogues say. Why is the text taken so lightly? Because from modern scholarship we learn that the Athenians were not serious about such things. The real source of that modern scholarly opinion is an argument made in the seventeenth and eighteenth centuries by men like Bayle, Gibbon, and Montesquieu, that Christianity was the source of intolerance. They consciously rationalized Greek and Roman politics in order to present it as a favorable contrast in matters of religion to modern nations so much affected by the religions founded on Biblical revelation. Thus the real charge against Socrates is ignored because we are influenced by earlier thinkers who knew what they were about. But we think we have founded our knowledge of the Greeks on scientific philology. The blindness to our own thought and to the text of Plato is fraught with consequences. The importance of religion and the critique of it in Plato is missed. This only supports the current easygoingness about the religious question about which I have spoken. The value of Plato as an articulator of problems we forget is thus lost. A curious contradiction in contemporary thought leads to the view that, on the one hand, the Athenians did not take the gods to be the most important beings and, on the other hand, that Socrates was conventionally pious. The text of the *Apology* teaches that Socrates was guilty as charged: that he did not believe in the gods of the city. And this is not a merely scholarly point, because the case of Athens and Socrates is typical, according to Plato. All cities must have gods, and all philosophers must doubt their existence. If this is the case, the rationalization of politics is impossible. The possibility of that rationalization is taken for granted in most of modern political thought. (Only Rousseau—the greatest modern reader of Plato—makes the rejection of that possibility an important part of his teaching. For this stand Rousseau is taken to be a crank.) And this belief is one of the most important and pervasive influences in contemporary politics. The alternative to it is obscured by apparent science. Just looking at Plato open-mindedly would free us from our prejudice.

Openness is the general principle in the study of texts. But it is a different kind of openness from that which is most praised today. Contemporary openness is based on closedness to the possibility of the truth of the thought of the past, whereas the openness required is one that can call into question our openness and the specific modern thought on which it is based. To achieve such an openness nothing more is required than deideoligization and the love of truth. There are no universally applicable rules of interpretation, for each author has different intentions and a different rhetoric. Each must be understood from within. He must be worn like a pair of glasses through which we see the world. It is unlikely that we shall be able to read many books in such a way, but the experience of one book profoundly read will teach more than many read lightly, because the most important experience is not the dazzling succession of ill-conceived ideas, but the recognition of seriousness. He who has read one book well is in a position to read any book, while he for whom books are easy currency is rendered incapable of living fully with one.

In all this what may seem most perverse is my apparent denigration of scholarship, particularly historical scholarship. Books have something to do with the time and the language in which they were written, and they are full of references which only the learned can understand. It is almost inconceivable that it should be argued that we are not greatly aided by all the research of the last ages. And I would agree that learning is a good thing, if it is not learning for its own sake and if that learning serves the understanding of the books instead of encouraging the use of the books as raw material for the scholar's system. Another maxim is that our learning should be guided strictly by the author's understanding. We should learn about history from Machiavelli; look to those authors to whom Machiavelli refers us; take seriously the teachings he takes seriously. He should be our preceptor, and we should follow his curriculum.

The first thing a student will observe is that Machiavelli is written in Italian. If he does not know Italian, he must learn it. There are translations, but one cannot trust them. But if he learns Italian as the translators learned Italian, he might as well not learn Italian. For example, none of the translators translates *virtu* as *virtue*, at least not uniformly. They say that it does not mean *virtue* in Machiavelli or in the Renaissance. When *virtu* seems to designate what the translator thinks virtue is, he renders it virtue. When it does not, he will use *ability, ingenuity*, or whatever. But Machiavelli uses the same word and actually plays on the traditional use to indicate his transvaluation of values. In one place he uses it three times in two sentences, designating radically different things and thus says something very shocking. But the translators use three or at least two different words, thereby destroying the teaching. The problem is not one of philology, but of the conventionalism of mind of the translators. They think Machiavelli could not mean what he says. Inaccurate translation reflects inaccuracy of understanding, the tyranny of the scholar's prejudice over the matter to which he should be subservient. To learn Italian for the sake of understanding Machiavelli as the translators understand him is a waste of time. Most of the important words Machiavelli uses can be understood by following his use of them, and to do that requires no sophisticated science, just a lot of work. Anyone who takes the trouble to study Rousseau's use of the expression *le peuple* will find that this great friend of the people means pretty much the same thing as does Plato when he uses *dēmos*: the hopelessly prejudiced many. Someone might retort that one has to know Plato to recognize that. But Rousseau himself refers the reader to Plato in the clearest way. And this is only another proof that it is not Rousseau's own time that is most helpful in understanding him. Plato is much more important for interpreting Rousseau than is Voltaire. The education required for studying Rousseau can be learned from Rousseau. And incidentally, one gets a better understanding of Plato from a man of Rousseau's caliber than one would from the most learned philologist. This is only indicative of how the study of one author can lead to a grasp of the tradition as a whole and entirely from within.

Our students must, then, learn languages, and that is not to their taste. But they must be guided by their philosophic concern in the study of langugages and not be carried away into the infinite labyrinths of philology. Far more important is that they keep thinking of the book of the world and comparing the words in the philosopher's book to the things in the world.

Similarly, Machiavelli talks about historical events and persons. Must we not know what happened in its fullness to see whether Machiavelli is right and how he interprets? But this presupposes that we have a true account against which to measure Machiavelli's account. In reality it comes down to accepting some modern historian's view as opposed to Machiavelli's. Moreover this supposes that Machiavelli's intention is to give an accurate historical account rather than to make a specific point for which he is willing to distort the facts. In *Prince* II Machiavelli speaks of two dukes of Ferrara as though they were the same. But a moment's reflection will prove that this is intentional, that he wishes to indicate that in solid, traditional states it makes little difference who rules. In III he speaks of Louis XII's invasions of Italy. In VII and XI he gives very different accounts of those invasions. Putting the three accounts together, one can see that Machiavelli wishes to show that Italian politics are controlled and corrupted by the Roman Catholic Church. He first presents Louis as an independent actor, and gradually reveals, to those who pay attention, that Louis was the dupe of Alexander VI. This history can be constructed internally, and most scholarly history would stand in the way of recognizing it.

Finally, in *The Prince*, Machiavelli refers to other books, most especially the Bible and Xenophon. One is expected to know their significance. It goes without saying that Machiavelli counted on more cultivated readers than can today be expected, and we must make every effort to be what he wanted us to be in order to teach us. But, again, to understand the Bible or Xenophon, we must begin by recovering what Machiavelli thought the traditional understanding and use of these books was. He refers not to the Bible of the higher criticism, but to the Bible of the believers and the Church. To know the Bible one must be familiar with its text as it is written and at least have some sense of what it means to believe. Then Machiavelli takes over from there. All the contemporary erudition about the Bible does not help us see Machiavelli's interesting use of it—for example, how he rewrites the story of David and Goliath, or his blasphemies about Moses founding a people. Likewise, classical studies have reassured us that Xenophon is simple and a bore, so Machiavelli's learning from him the two forms of liberality—the legitimate, using other people's property, the illegitimate, using one's own—loses its sense. This passage in Machiavelli is essential for understanding his agreement and disagreement with Greek political philosophy. Machiavelli should teach us the wonders of Xenophon, whereas some classical scholarship has given Machiavelli a lesson as to Xenophon's defects.

Study of the texts in this way is an endless task; but so is the study of nature, and the two studies go hand in hand and are almost the same. This is the truly liberal study. One would, of course, ultimately become very learned by means of it. But the learning would have a coherent and authentic character, one related to the highest purposes of life. Great books are full of hidden references and quotes which reveal themselves only to initiates. But there is no short cut to the initiation: The route goes only by way of the ever-deepening reflection on the books as they relate to the problems of the world.

An example of the kind of awareness which is not immediately accessible on the surface of the books, which is dependent on a history that emerges immanently from the books, can be drawn from Tocqueville. Tocqueville often is called a conservative and is almost always contrasted with Rousseau, the radical and revolutionary. These are categories—simple ones, ones that seem almost to be of perennial common sense—used in academic and popular discourse. History comes to the aid of these categories to explain Tocqueville's position as a result of reaction to the French Revolution, his aristocratic origins, etc. as opposed to that of Rousseau, the optimist of the Enlightenment, the resentful poor boy. All of this is very plausible and such explanations have a particularly exhilarating effect on the modern mind. But the more one really knows, the less one finds them helpful. I had always accepted this interpretation of Tocqueville, and only recently, forced by facts, my reflections have begun to take a different turn. Tocqueville rarely mentions Rousseau and speaks denigratingly of the *philosophes*. But, while studying *Emile*, I had to teach *Democracy in America*. On coming to the passage on the role of compassion in democracies I was compelled to recognize that it was based on the discussion of compassion in the *Emile*. Not only is the argument the same, but Tocqueville makes the same literary reference, to La Fontaine, as does Rousseau. The latter cannot be an accidental connection, for it is so idiosyncratically Rousseauean. Now this is not a minor question. Compassion is Rousseau's supplement to self-interest as the social bond. This is his correction of the natural right teaching of Hobbes and Locke. Tocqueville agrees with Rousseau that egalitarian society brings forth this disposition and that it is what tempers the selfishness of democratic prin-

136

ALLAN BLOOM

ciples of right. Beginning from there, I looked back over the whole scheme which Tocqueville used to analyze American democracy and realized how great a debt he owes Rousseau. The alternative facing modern man, according to Tocqueville, is egalitarian democracy or egalitarian tyranny. And this is precisely Rousseau's teaching. Aristocracies for both are dead; they were unjust but contained a certain real nobility which is likely to disappear in democracies. Thus the political project for Tocqueville is to preserve freedom in equality and a tincture of nobility in democracy. Such is also Rousseau's intention. What is the way of achieving freedom in equality? Small communities with religious foundations. That is straight Rousseau. The concentration on the size of community was Rousseau's restoration of a classical theme within the context of modern political thought which denied its significance. And the civil religion described in the *Social Contract* closely parallels Tocqueville's descriptions of and prescriptions for religion in democracy. Tocqueville on the family, the role of women, the arts, the habits of mind, and even rhetoric is derivative from Rousseau. In his description of an Indian he once saw Tocqueville even echoes Rousseau's ultimate doubt about the superiority of civilized life for happiness, this again as over against Hobbes and Locke. Tocqueville looked at the king in America, whom Locke said was worse clothed, housed, and fed than the day laborer in England, and asked, as did Rousseau, whether the crucial question was put by modern thought: Is that king less happy?

One could say much more about this intimate relation between Rousseau and Tocqueville. But I limit myself to indicating the harmony of their views. Why then does Tocqueville not acknowledge his great teacher and why does he appear so moderate? One must look to his addressees and his explicit intention. He writes to reconcile the well-born and the well-educated to democratic principles and life, in order that democracy will not be torn apart by the opposition of its most talented elements and will be tempered by their leadership and participation. Rousseau was a red flag waved before such men. It was not vanity but prudence that caused Tocqueville to hide his debt to Rousseau. The more moderate tone is partly illusory, for Rousseau was much more moderate in expectation than is often thought. Moreover, the principles of the rights of man, revolutionary in the *ancien régime*, were no longer so after the revolution. That debate was over. Tocqueville's business was to make them work politically. I do not argue that Tocqueville is simply the same as Rousseau; but the more I think about it, the difficulty is more on the side of differentiating them than of assimilating them.

To conclude, I should like to say a word about Rousseau himself and the way he should be read. It is often noted that Rousseau is the philosopher who attacked philosophy. This is a blatant contradiction and would seem to stem from the vain love of paradox. But on living with Rousseau, one becomes aware that he attacks philosophy but praises Socrates. That would seem to be a continuation of the same paradox, for Socrates, the founder of political philosophy, did nothing but defend philosophy and try to make it appear divine. However, Rousseau makes it clear that Socrates lived in a world in which philosophy was new, where it was thought to be dangerous and it played no role in public life. Philosophy needed a defense in order to be preserved; it had to be made to appear to be good for political life. But the situation had changed in Rousseau's time. Philosophy was the rage; it had become the adviser to enlightened despots and the comforter and helper of the peoples. Philosophy was becoming a tool of the prejudices and a servant of the selfish passions. For the sake of political virtue and the preservation of true philosophy, the public philosophy had to be attacked. The very opposition in speech between Socrates and Rousseau is indicative of the profoundest agreement in thought. Rousseau's critique of modernity—which means us—comes to light only by way of such reflections.

It is obvious that much stands in the way of the education I propose. I have outlined some of the most notable obstacles.

Its actualization seems almost impossible—except that it is so simple, so available, and so charming. I have found that young Americans are seduced by the discovery of books—in a book-drenched society—books unadorned with alien paraphernalia. They are thirsty for clarity and inspiration, and they can find both so readily at hand. This is my hope, for almost all that is institutional stands in the way of the study of books. Such an education, whatever its other results, gives the students an experience of the possibilities of human greatness and of community based on shared thought that cannot fail to alter their expectations from politics.

destructively, by identifying several senses in which "the history of political philosophy" need not and should not be
taught to the next generation, because these senses of the term
seem to me to lack sufficient precision of meaning. My hope
that I shall not be charged with wanting it taught in these very
senses rises briefly above its initially low level.

To begin with, then, I do not think that political philosophy possesses a unified and narratable history, or that the efforts of those who may disagree with me to prove otherwise
are likely to provide legitimate paradigms for the coming
paideia. I say this with some regret and even a sense of ingrati-
tude, for the classical work of G. H. Sabine had an enormously illuminating and liberating effect upon me when I was
an undergraduate of nineteen. But that was long ago and far
away, and the next generation would not thank me for ex-
pecting them to start wherever I was then. I do not mean
merely that nobody will ever again read the work of Sabine in
the year 1943. His was, I now think, a survey volume of genius, and I still encourage undergraduates to read it—not least
because survey volumes today seem to be written with the
aim of avoiding genius at all costs. But, as I have argued at
length elsewhere, any historian who tries to provide himself
with a model of political philosophies as the products of historical processes is bound to ask the question whether what he
is studying is in fact the record of a continuous activity with a
history of its own. Breathe for one moment the words "second order," and the possibility must arise that political philosophy is what happens when people reflect upon their political languages and that political languages are what social
beings assemble from a multitude of sources to articulate and
coordinate a multitude of activities. All this is simply too
diverse and disorderly—being of the groundstuff of history
itself—to have a single evolving pattern of history. The questions with which political philosophers come to deal may
perhaps be perennial—I do not intend to deny this, though I
do think we need critical means of determining when to say it
and when not—but precisely when they are, they cannot be

historical. There may indeed be a history made up of philosophers reading and responding to other philosophers—they are certainly to be observed doing this—but at the same time there is, far closer to the grassroots, a history of philosophers not being philosophers twenty-four hours a day and receiving information and inputs, both philosophical and non-philosophical, from beings inhabiting the same social and historical moments as those in which they happen to live. If political philosophy exists in the world of concrete history, it does not have a history altogether its own, and its attempts to provide itself with one are only a part of the story of what has happened. To descend from the question of kind to the question of degree, it may be added that political philosophy has probably been less successful at providing itself with an autonomous and continuous history than Christian dogma or scientific discovery; these, even the former, got further out of the marketplace (I use this last term in a Baconian rather than a Macphersonian sense).

What I have been saying depends upon a certain model of what political philosophy is, and how it is generated in society and history. About that model I may have occasion to say more, but my present point may be made without it, by suggesting that the notion that there is "a" history of political philosophy disappears once we entertain the possibility that such philosophy may have been generated, and had a history, in more than one independently existing and unrelated civilization. In this book we are not discussing (though the next generation very possibly may) the significance for us of political thought in the civilizations of Asia; but once we suppose that Wang Yang-ming may have been as important to the young Mao as Herbert Spencer, or that Augustan England and Tokugawa Japan may have arrived at interestingly comparable notions concerning the interrelations of land, commerce, war, and virtue, we shall be forced to acknowledge that no single history of political thought or philosophy can possibly be written; for here are at least two such histories, which took shape and existed in complete separation from

one another until the coming of the black ships. And each of
these, I am prepared to argue, both can and must be further
dissolved by criticism into an indefinite number of discrete
historical phenomena, the discontinuities between which are
at least of equal importance with the continuities.

It is the historical intelligence which is destructive of histories so conceived, just as it can discern that most of the historians described by Professor Bloom were very bad historians indeed. If the practicing historian rejects the notion of
writing an overall "history of political philosophy" at a level
higher than that of the textbook survey, he will *a fortiori* show
even greater skepticism when faced by majestic schemes of
general development through which political philosophy is
supposed to have passed. He will not argue for exposing the
coming generation to the view that political philosophy has
passed from the city-state to the universal community to the
nation-state, from feudal to bourgeois to socialist, from the
ancient tradition of natural law to the modern heresy of natural right, or to any other of the intellectual hippogriffs still
seen to lurch, entangled in their own coils, across the floor at
political science conventions. These were at their simplest,
models, and at their richest, myths: insights into and symbols
of aspects of reality, like the hippogriff itself; it was only when
they were imposed upon the historiography of the actual, of
experience and event, that they ceased to be myths and became monsters instead. The historian is not in the monster-
making business, so long as what he wants to know about
political philosophy is simply what he wants to know about
any other recorded human activity, namely what it was that
happened and how. None of the monsters I have mentioned
was the work of a historian; all were the work of social philosophers of one kind and another, who thought they knew
enough history for their purposes.

And it is here that we encounter the central problem of re-
lating the discipline of history to the *paideia* of political philosophers. The historian's purpose may very well be somewhat critical and negative, and markedly non-imperialist. He

may aver that he has no desire to convert political philosophers into historians—even historians of philosophy—and that he is offering only to teach them enough history to keep them out of Operation Frankenstein. But it is precisely on those interfaces where the practitioners of one discipline think they know all they need of another that Frankenstein is found begetting monsters in his sleep; and it is not enough to teach them their second discipline with negative and critical intentions, since the apparent humility of thinking they know all they need may well turn out to be the fatal step into hubris. On the other hand, it is futile to suppose that teaching the coming generation no history will prevent them supposing that they know some and engaging in a variety of pseudohistorical enterprises. Frankenstein did not die in the Arctic; he was picked up by a vessel of the Vanderdecken and Ahab Line and his monsters roam the world to this day. Nor, when the parable is applied to the case before us, could he altogether help acting as he did and does; the political philosopher of today is an intensely historical animal, conscious of inhabiting history even when he rejects it and bound to include historical statements among those which he makes and implies. I do not mean by this that every statement he makes must be a historical statement, but I do mean that if we do not want bad history as part of our political philosophy, we must do something to help the philosophers abstain from producing it.

But I have been urging that the attempt to provide political philosophy with a history will not be a sufficient means of reaching even this modest goal, and it is inherent in my argument that to think of history as an auxiliary or ancillary skill for the philosopher will not solve the problem of the interface, which is the problem of Frankenstein. We have to seek means of making the intensification of historical understanding part of the philosophical enterprise itself, without encouraging it to take over the enterprise as a whole. It has been suggested—and I think it can, within the proper limits, be maintained—that such a means can be looked for in the historical interpretation of texts, though this must be carried out by criticism and not by Professor Bloom's strange blend of innocence and esoteric initiation. Here, it is important to note, what is proposed is not that we should study the history of political philosophy, but that we should study political philosophy historically; a very different thing, and one which brings us much closer to the problem of historicism. I propose now to confront that problem head on, by considering why it is that to admit the notion of texts to the argument sentences the political philosopher to be an inhabitant of history, without sentencing him to think historically for more than part of his time.

To speak of texts is one way of admitting that the philosopher is not isolated from his own kind. He is aware of the utterances of other political philosophers, and indeed of other political beings of many kinds whose articulate speech-acts constitute inputs to his consciousness. In saying what he says he responds to what he supposes them to have said, and the interpretation of other men's speech-acts forms so large a part of his specialized activity that political philosophy has become a thing which he studies at least as much as a thing which he practices. It is possible to deplore this, or at least to set limits to its desirability; but it is a fact, and means must be found of coping with it as a fact. Because the philosopher spends much of his time responding to what others are supposed to have said, political philosophy may be spoken of as a "conversation," a "tradition," a "dialogue" going on over time, and is a historical activity in the sense that it possesses a historical dimension.

Where there is conversation there are two speakers, and where there are two speakers neither has complete command over what is being said, even by himself. Let me hasten to add that there are limits to the extent to which political philosophy is a conversation even when there are two speakers. It may be supposed that whenever a political philosopher says anything, he is in part responding to something which he takes another to have said; but should Alter object "I didn't say that," or "I didn't mean that," it would not be improper for Ego to retort "I don't care whether you did or not; all I wanted to say was that if such and such a proposition were to be enunciated, my comment would be such and such." From that point on, Ego is emancipated from his conversation with Alter; the speech-acts which he now performs, the language games into which he now enters, are contingent upon the obtaining of certain conditions which he may have specified quite correctly, and which do not in any event depend upon what Alter said or meant to say. Ego has entered into a hypothetical world of his own specification, self-legitimizing in the sense that the specifications he constructs may specify and include his reasons for constructing them; and the exercise may be a most valuable one for Ego himself and for anyone who may happen to be listening. Even Alter may learn something to his advantage from what must necessarily be something of a monologue on Ego's part, and it is not inconceivable that the conversation which Ego broke off may at some time be resumed in a more beneficial form. It is the Socratic assumption that it always will be, though we do well to be skeptical of any man's pretensions to play Socrates.

Now when philosophers say that they do not wish to be entrapped into historicism, they often mean, in part, that they wish to preserve the freedom to play Ego in the little mono-drama I have just recounted; and this is indeed a freedom it is important to preserve. It was annoying for Alter that Ego gave him the alternatives of withdrawing from the conversation or remaining to listen to it as a monologue conducted by Ego within parameters he had constructed for himself; but Ego may have had something more important in mind than finding out what Alter wished to talk about and talking about that. He should be free to break off even the most bilateral of conversations, and what is more, he is free to do so. No non-coercive means of stopping philosophic disputants behaving like Ego has yet been found, and the commonest difficulty is the relatively trivial one of getting them to admit, even to themselves, that this is what they are doing. I have next to show in greater depth why it is that philosophers should and do have the freedom to operate upon the utterances of other philosophers, irrespective of their historical reality; but I aim also to show why it is that to do so will not always be an appropriate or even a possible strategy.

Ego behaved as he did because he sought the power and the freedom to determine what he was going to talk about. The affirmation, "If so and so were said, then the reply would be such and such," carried with it the plain implication, "And I don't want to discuss anything else." The erection of a set of conditions—intellectually scrupulous though it may have been—was a power play, a bid to set the rules of the game to be played. Ego acted in this way, let us suppose, because he was aware of the muddle-ridden character of ordinary language, and knew how much of this confusion arose from its character as conversation, in which two or more persons are and have been talking at cross-purposes. He had reached a decision as to what it was he wanted to talk about, and he declared that decision; whereof he could or would not speak, thereof was he silent, and he compelled Alter to be silent also. Such, one might say, is language in its Hobbesian state of nature, except that the clarificatory monologue is the state towards which philosophers (Plato was not an exception) normally desire to lead all discourse; it is their means of escaping from the ordinariness of ordinary language, even if this is only escape into second-order talk about ordinary language. But it is perhaps a more common experience for us to find that we do not yet know what the muddles are, or even whether there are any in the part of the swamp we are traversing. The appropriate strategy now is not to terminate or explode the conversation, but to continue it. Ego and Alter may say to one another, "Where shall we get to if we go on talking like this? We must go cautiously ahead and find out." It may happen that their existing, ordinary, language turns out adequate to their purposes, and does not lead them into insoluble muddles. In that event, the distinction between first- and second-order language will, to some extent, fail to develop, but it does not seem on that account that the enterprise to which they committed themselves will prove to have been unphilosophical. If one side of the philosophical enterprise is to discover whereof one can speak, another is to discover what in the foggy blue morning—to quote the immortal Pogo—one has been talking about. If Ego and Alter succeed in carrying on conversation, each will be engaged in discovering what the other says and means to say, and—as an inescapable corollary—what he says and means to say himself.

It is the presence of what we mean by ordinary language that gives political philosophy its character as history. Strictly speaking, the language in which it is conducted is academic and extraordinary, and it might be better to call it a tradition of discourse. But it shares with ordinary language and other kinds of tradition the characteristic that it is a continuum of behavior, compounded of material from many sources and available to many users in such a way that no one of them has unlimited power over it. Perhaps the key characteristic of tradition is that no single transmitter has complete knowledge or complete control of the messages he either receives or transmits; there is always an element of the implicit and perhaps the contradictory, which must escape his attention at any single moment of transmission. This does not deny his capacity to perform acts of unilateral clarification like Ego's; it merely provides the context in which such acts of self-liberation become necessary and possible. There must be a river before you can swim upstream; you cannot be purifying all the dialect all the time.

The theorem of linguistic continuity also presupposes the importance of Alter, as the most recent transmitter to whose use of language we respond in ways that must be dialectically related to it, but who was himself behaving in the same way towards some other transmitter before him. The chain of transmitters must formally be thought of as open-ended and immemorial; in the continuum of discourse called political philosophy it is, for complex and fascinating reasons, rendered visible and apparent over a time-span of up to two and a half thousand years, and can at any moment be short-circuited in such ways that we find ourselves responding with high immediacy to Alters who lived in Athens or the State of Lu as long ago as that. But if we are prepared to say that the relation between Ego and Alter is a historical one, on the grounds that they occupy distinguishable moments in the same continuum or tradition of behavior and respond to one another's attempts to use and modify it, then this relation must be a historical one, whether the distance separating them in time, space, and context is very large or very small. It is the use of language—of language not perfectly controlled by its users—that constitutes the historicity of political philosophy, as of many another activity.

I hope I need not stress much further that to say this is not to fix a historicist straitjacket upon what Ego was doing when he exploded his conversation with Alter. He was at that point trying to establish the formal conditions under which language could be used to say certain things, and his assertion that he knew what could be done under specified conditions need in no way depend for its truth or falsity upon acts of historical knowledge. He established tests and appealed to criteria which were valid within the limits to which the conditions necessary for their validation could be made clear. To talk about the extent of this clarification was not simply to continue the tradition of discourse, or more sophisticatedly to discuss the conditions under which it was being continued. Nor was it immediately necessary to discuss the possibility that the language in use for purposes of specification contained unstated implications being borne along as part of the language continuum. The immediate necessity was to find out whether language was behaving as it had been said that it would behave, and only after that to begin considering why it was not, the answer to which might or might not have to do with the historicity of language. Ego would be on safe ground in affirming that the historicity of language did not immediately concern him, and that he hoped to establish conditions and a methodology under which it never would. It can be affirmed with equal force, however, that his enterprise was being undertaken at a certain historical moment and was helping to constitute that moment, but that, given the presumption of the language continuum, he should not hope to command everything that happened, or that he was doing, at that moment. His experiment, considered as a speech-act, would be heard by, and communicated to, people who were not committed to its original enterprise; his specification of conditions would be heard under conditions which it did not specify. The validity of the experiment would not be diminished when it was reabsorbed by a non-experimental universe, but it would be so reabsorbed all the same. Ego need not worry about this; he should obey the First Law of Methodology and do his job; but his job would never be the whole of what he was doing.

Ego, then, has an unlimited right, but not an unlimited power, to set himself free from his interlocutor in a conversation or a tradition, or—what amounts to the same thing—from the uncontrolled historicity of his language. Let me now proceed to consider how this affects the problem of how far his understanding of other people's thought needs to be a historical understanding. I have already insisted that any linguistic relation between two persons can be thought of as a historical relation, and the fact that the historical distance between them may be as great as two and a half millennia only serves to highlight the problems of historicity which the relationship involves. We do in fact find ourselves in philosophical conversation with Plato, the author of the Book of Job, and Confucius, and while there are different ways of accounting for the fact, there is no need to defend or apologize for it. We may say that a great tradition, or a historical continuity, connects twentieth-century Westerners with ancient Greeks and Hebrews, and if it is harder to say this of ancient Chinese, we may plausibly predict of the next generation either that they will have connected themselves with the grand continuity that descends from Confucians, Taoists, and Legalists, or that they will have developed still further our interest in the varieties of historical experience that have produced and transmitted the ideas of Plato or of Han Fei Tzu. As for hard-nosed operationalist Ego, we have given him liberty to withdraw from the historical conversation whenever and insofar as he is able to, and we owe him no explanation of our reasons for remaining in it. He is not welcome to this congregation in his favorite role of Lesser Inquisitor. Let him do his job, and we will listen to him.

We may say of our predecessors in the history of political philosophy that they are linked to us by tradition, by the continuity or the diversity of history, or by the fact that the questions they discussed were classical, perennial, or timeless, and are still discussed by us. I myself do not particularly wish to say any of these things, though I am equally not concerned to deny any of them. It seems enough, and more important, to make the merely humanist point that when we are able to receive and decipher a transmission from any predecessor in our common enterprise, the reasons for receiving it are potentially so numerous and diverse that they do not need to be spelled out in advance. If the next generation plans to remain human at all—and, by the way, some of them don't—there is no human resource which they can afford to neglect.

But on the premise that we are using "ordinary language," or a "tradition of discourse," it must follow that Ego is receiving from his predecessors and interlocutors messages whose diversity is yet to be controlled and may never be brought under control altogether. Speech-acts and utterances in political philosophy, when viewed as historical phenomena, must be considered as multidimensional. There must be a diversity of contexts in which, a diversity of levels on which, they may be and have been interpreted; and the content of any given message can be exclusively specified only under conditions which are experimental rather than historical. It was the endeavor of Ego in the monodrama to substitute experiment for history, and he could enjoy only a specific and limited success in doing so. But while, at his end of the transmission, he is at liberty to reshape the message being received into the form in which he desires to receive and respond to it, there may be going on elsewhere in the continuum—and he cannot altogether ignore that there may be going on—the effort to reconstitute the message as it may have been at the moment of emission, or at any intervening moment of transmission. The historian is bugging the time-stream and has interposed his own unscrambler. We cannot deny that he is there; we must find him his own job to do.

One thinks of the historian as endeavoring to discover Alter's original meaning and intention, and feeding statements concerning this into Ego's already overburdened sensorium. In point of fact, it seems unduly restrictive to think of him as overwhelmingly concerned with Alter's intended meaning, central as this may be to his problem. If political philosophy both emerges from and remains within a universe of ordinary speech, it is true of any statement—Ego's as well as Alter's—that it can be both made and understood in a number of contexts and on a number of levels. It is also true that the speaker's problem may be to discover and determine his own intention as to the context and level in and on which he desires to speak and be understood. We may go further. It is possible that his intention emerges as that of speaking and being understood in several contexts and on several levels; it is possible that the determination of his intention was never finally accomplished by him, and can never be finally accomplished by anyone else; and it is probable, rather than merely possible, that the meaning he intended his statement to bear was not identical with the meaning assigned to it by any one of the chain of transmitters—disciples, opponents, critics, scholars, historians—who may have conveyed the statement to Ego. The historian of ideas bedevils the philosopher, not merely by pointing out what some statement which the latter desires to use may have meant to the author from whom he receives it, but by pointing out the embarrassing richness of meanings which the statement may have and/or has borne to the author himself and to any other historical actor involved in its operations.

I have consistently depicted Ego as a highly analytical and

operational sort of philosopher, who desires only to take up some speech-act that has come to his attention and play language-games with it. I have done this not in order to suggest that all philosophers are like this—though the type is common enough—but in order to widen the gap between Ego and Alter to the point where Ego may quite legitimately say that Alter's intentions are no concern of his. In reality, of course, Ego may be a humanist, genuinely concerned to maintain and affirm the value of his dialogues with the dead; or he may be a historicist, convinced that Alter's thought, and his own, and the relations between them, can be understood only by reconstituting each in its historicity. In such cases it really will matter to him that Alter's true name was Plato or Hobbes, and it really will matter that the utterance he desires to explore was one which Plato or Hobbes not only made, but intended to be understood in the sense which he desires to explore. But I have deliberately sought to define a situation in which Ego may detach Alter's utterance from Alter's intention so completely that it no longer matters to him who Alter was, in which case the most that can be said is that it might be best to stop using Alter's proper name. If you really do not care whether or not Plato said this, a name so potent is probably better omitted. Supposing a situation as extreme as this, however, what significance, if any, will still attach to the intervention of a historian between Ego and Alter?

Some might argue at this point that if Ego does not desire to use Alter's name, he had better not use his words either. Words, they might say, are phenomena so far historical that a complex speech-act can never be finally divested of the meanings attached to it by the original utterance or accumulated in the process of transmission. Ego had better render Alter's speech into a notation of his own, if he really needs to get away from Alter altogether and perform a speech-act under conditions perfectly controlled. But I have premised that Ego's attempt to withdraw from the universe of ordinary speech into a laboratory universe of his own is always to be encouraged, but can never be more than provisionally successful; and what we have to do is consider the historian's intervention in the light of this supposition. It will mean that Ego may indeed rephrase Alter's speech to the point where Alter and his speech-act disappear, but that outside the laboratory Alter and his speech will still be historically present and operative, and that the historian will be in there, scrambling and unscrambling, with them. What then is his value, or his nuisance value, to Ego?

In the first place it may be pointed out that historical criticism is a potent means of slaying monsters. "Man's world," wrote Collingwood, "is infested by sphinxes: demonic beings of mixed and monstrous nature which ask him riddles and eat him if he cannot answer them,"[1] and while some of these sphinxes are unfortunately real, others are phantasmata—monsters begotten in the sleep of reason—who will disappear if we point out not so much the right answer as the nonsensicality of the question. To point out that a given interpretation of an utterance could not have been its author's intention on grounds of historical anachronism may lead us to enquire into the reasons why such an interpretation should have been assigned to the utterance at any subsequent moment, including the present, at which, let us suppose, Ego is proposing to analyze the utterance as bearing that meaning. If he discovers, thanks to historical criticism, that there has never yet been any good reason for supposing that it meant that, he may well be moved to enquire once again what reason he has for so supposing. If he has a good reason—especially one non-historical in character—historical criticism will not invalidate it; on the contrary, it may reinforce it. But it will, somewhat indirectly, oblige him to restate his reason and gain added certainty that his sphinx is not a phantasma. So much for historical criticism in its negative form, when it leads to the conclusion, "Hobbes did not mean what it suits you to suppose his words mean." The next step is to ask the question, "Why exactly does it suit you to suppose so?" But it is implicit in the assumption I have been making that historical criticism—or rather reconstruction—is less likely to operate negatively, excluding the meaning which Ego desires to impose on the words, than positively, drawing attention to the embarrassing richness of other meanings which they could have and have borne at one time and another. In this respect its value to Ego is surely that it vastly expands his consciousness of the variety of language-games which he may play, while conveying a salutary reminder of the variety of language-games which his readers may and will assume—whatever his declared intentions to the contrary—that he has been playing. We return to the point at which Ego's exit from the world of history into that of experiment is seen to be laudable but never complete, and it may be suggested that we have isolated some ways in which historical criticism can help provide dialogue between the historical and the experimental modes of his activity.

In making what seem to me legitimate concessions to historicism, I have been trying to point out that the non-historical statement does not become the less non-historical when we discover that nevertheless it has a history and is in history. I have been implying that the specification of conditions of validation is sufficient to erect the laboratory and legitimize its experiments. Some may not find this satisfactory, but I will presume that the question is likely to remain debatable and unresolved, at least to the point where we are not required to resolve it for the benefit of the coming generation (which is likely to reopen it, whatever we say). But a perfectly evident corollary is that Ego's choice of what experiments he will make, what meanings he will choose to impute to utterances, what laboratories he will build, takes place in the historical world and precedes his exit from it. To emphasize this is more important than to debate the completeness of his exit from its determining conditions. It is while he is still in the historical world, considering what non-historical operations he will perform upon it, that a critical knowledge of history seems most likely to discipline and reinforce his proceedings; and if we emphasize that his exit from history may not be complete and cannot be permanent, we do so in

of ends, so that not all the consequences of his acts will be those he can foresee, intend, or desire. Once again, we have not obliged him to think historically while he is constructing his thought-experiments, but we have trained him to resume thinking historically in proportion as the conditions specified in the experiment cease to obtain. Now these two sets of advantages can be thought of as operating in the world as it appears to a humanist, in which the resources of humanity are spread out over time, and dialogue, or relatively unmediated communication, between minds widely separated in history is a thing to be desired. The situation I have been describing is one in which the philosopher learns that he and his method share the world with other beings and other methods, some of which may be induced to counterpoint, limit, and enrich the operations he practices. In the world thus described there is a plurality of powers and there are relations between these powers, and the political biases of my description may be said to be liberal. I do not reject this definition; I reject only that antiliberal polemic which distorts the word "liberal" by applying it to the world in which Ego operates unchecked. I have been trying to check him, and grant him his liberty.

But in essaying a humanist projection, I have also been seeking ways of making legitimate concessions to historicism. There is a historicist projection of the world in which the historicity of everything is at all points the condition of its being, and to which it would be highly relevant that the dialogue of Ego and Alter could be arranged so that each discovered his historicity. Now, at one level the objection to historicism is that it obliges us to think historically when we desire to think in other ways; at another, the objection is that it exposes us to rule by a new caste of philosopher-kings who claim to know more about our historicity than we do ourselves, and so much about everyone's historicity that they have power over it and them. For those of us who object as strenuously to Leninist philosopher-kings as we do to operationalist ones, and for the same reasons, I have emphasized the historical context of Ego's experiments in order to prevent him from becoming

the latter kind of usurper (or Sphinx), and his freedom to perform experiments in history in order to defend him against
the former kind. That is a modest, Whiggish, commonsensi-
cal contribution to the debate between scientificist and historicist, a debate which I well know can be carried on at much
higher levels of refinement and which looks like being so carried on by the next generation of political philosophers. Since
I am a historian of an Anglo-American tradition which acknowledges its debt to humanism somewhat more freely than
its debt to historicism, I have chosen to adopt a humanist approach to the borders of historicism, and to show how a historical sensitivity thus generated might be used to reach an
accommodation with the reigning oligarchy of scientific
experimentalists, and even to make them want one.

But the tradition from which I speak has enemies to the left,
and a holistic or totalitarian historicism is notoriously one of
them. Presuming as I do that the next generation will once
again be exposed to seduction and abduction from that
quarter—from bad Hegelianism, bad Marxism, and worse
Sartreanism—I would lay a good deal of emphasis on the
view that an essential ingredient of coping with the historicist
is the ability to know your own history and to know and
conduct yourself in it. Indeed, I will offer it as dogma that if
the next generation of political philosophers is historically ignorant and historically incompetent, it will be hopelessly vulnerable to the holistic scientists of the right and the holistic
historicists of the left, who are more than capable of combining against it. Frankenstein has many names and faces. But at
the same time there is a legitimate and valuable historicism, as
there are highly valuable forms of all three of the philosophies
whose proper names I used a moment ago; and having spent
my time in trying to show how much merit there is in viewing all kinds of political philosophy in their history, I should
conclude by laying some emphasis on the prevalence of a
political philosophy which is essentially a viewing of history.
This stems from pre-modern roots, which are found wherever the tradition, or the republic, or the national state, or the

revolution—all of which are modes of political association—is presented as having a history and facing problems of existence in it. It develops toward that modernity in which it is said that the political association is a historical animal and the individual's very consciousness of himself a historical consciousness, which determines the modes of his political and historical action. We may wish to repudiate this, for it has many grave inconveniences; but it does not appear that we can afford to neglect it. For one thing, it has developed a highly complex and subtle language, which is predominant outside our own tradition and wherever the angels are not Angles. We need to learn this language—I speak it very haltingly myself—and if we are not to be taken captive by it, we need one of our own, in which our awareness of our historicity is differently articulated. I have argued, then, both that the coming political philosopher will need to know how to think historically and that his thought will need a historicist dimension. In large measure I have argued this on adversary and disputatious grounds, but I would like to conclude by stressing my sense of the enrichment which such kinds of awareness may bring to his understanding of what the philosophical enterprise is, and which—even though they little note nor long remember what we say here—may help to rescue the next generation from the various forms of tyranny, technocracy, and tedium which, as usual, threaten to afflict it.

1. R. G. Collingwood, *The New Leviathan* (Oxford: Clarendon Press, 1947), p. 12.

POLITICAL DECISION-MAKING
AND POLITICAL EDUCATION

MICHAEL WALZER

In a democratic state, every citizen has political decisions to make. I don't mean only the decision to vote or not to vote, to support the Democrats or Republicans, to attend this meeting or sign that petition. There is a deeper level of deciding that I want to talk about, which has to do with the relation of the people to their political leaders. It is a special feature of democratic government that the experiences of leaders are not alien to ordinary citizens. There is no social distance; there are no mysteries of state. With only a modest imaginative effort, the citizen can put himself in the place of his elected representative. Because he can do that, and commonly does it, he engages in what I want to call (pretentiously, so as to suggest a certain kind of democratic pretension) anticipative and retrospective decision-making. He asks, "What would I do in his place?" and then, later on, he asks, "Would I have done what he did?" In a democracy, decisions are anticipated before they are made and reviewed after they are made, and these anticipations and retrospections play a large part in determining all those subsequent actions—voting, contributing money, demonstrating—to which political scientists normally devote their attention. Vicarious decision-making precedes and follows actual decision-making. In our minds, if not in fact, we imitate the Aristotelian ideal: We rule and are ruled in turn. We decide and we (usually, but not always) abide by the decisions of others.

It's not the case, then, as elitist writers have argued, that citizens merely reaffirm or reject their leaders at periodic

MICHAEL WALZER

intervals. They are, or large numbers of them are, engaged continually in another sort of activity which, because it is entirely a mental activity and has no immediate effects, is likely to make us smile: They are deciding whether or not to recognize Communist China, maintain troops in Europe, establish price and wage controls, and so on. It is this kind of decision-making that opinion pollsters try to capture, though without always appreciating its playful character. For our purposes, it is important to stress, first, that this is a peculiarly democratic form of play, and second, that it underlies the more serious work of citizens. We steal a march upon our leaders; then we second-guess them—and these two forms of democratic kibbitzing are crucial to our reflective judgments of their conduct. Indeed, political judgments might best be conceived as second-guessed decisions. When we say that such and such an action was wrong, one of the things we mean is that, granting the difficulties of the case and the tensions of the moment, we would have (or hope we would have) decided differently.

I want to argue that those of us who are involved in political education should pay attention to anticipative and retrospective decision-making. The study of politics should have this purpose: It should help ordinary citizens reflect upon the most important matters of state. It should prepare leaders, would-be leaders, and vicarious leaders—which is to say, it should prepare all of us—for the democratic business of taking stands and shaping policies. Political education cannot aim merely at explanation and foresight, as if politics were someone else's business, while we, the students, were scientific observers, having previously been casual spectators, and nothing more. Politics is our own (real and vicarious) activity, and it would be odd if we were to speak of ourselves only in the third person and make predictions as to our future conduct. It is important, of course, that we be able to think in some systematic way about the conduct of others, of our allies and adversaries in the political arena. That is a matter of orienting ourselves politically, of understanding the background conditions of decision-making. But the goal of orientation is action, and the relevant action is *making up one's mind*. There is a sense, I suppose, in which political philosophers and political scientists don't have to make up their minds; they can pursue understanding forever, studying issues from every possible perspective, holding all the elements of decision-making in indefinite suspension. But citizens must come down on one side or another. If they are ordinary citizens and not office-holders, they can make up their minds more than once, and they can change sides. But if they withdraw from the business of deciding, they cease in some important sense to be citizens, and the peculiar resonances of democratic politics yield to an ominous silence. (It is as if the opinion pollsters, making their daily rounds, were to encounter only men and women who quietly insisted, "I don't know.")

We all have pictures in our heads of the decision-making process, and I will examine two of these pictures later on. But first it is necessary to say something about a recent argument in political science which holds that the pictures shaped by vicarious decision-making don't usefully describe the actual processes of government. If that were true, it would be difficult indeed to fix upon the proper form of political education, or even to begin to understand how democratic government might work. Now, the pictures in our heads always involve a particular person (someone like ourselves) confronting a number of options, collecting information, consulting other (similar) people, and eventually, with whatever hesitation and nervousness, *deciding*. The moment of decision is and will probably remain a mystery; the picture nevertheless suggests the existence of a rational political or moral agent. And this is obviously appropriate to the anticipations and retrospections of ordinary citizens. If I decide to recognize Communist China, it is clear (attending now to the political circumstances of my choice and not to my psychological history) that I could have done otherwise; last week, perhaps, I decided to refuse recognition.

But governmental decisions, we are told, have a different

provenance. They are determined by bureaucratic operating procedures and bureaucratic interests. The individual decision-maker operates in an extremely constricted and constricting environment. He never confronts the actual range of options available to him or finds room for maneuver and rational choice, because the information that reaches him is distorted by the media through which it is collected; because his advisors are never "open" to the issues but narrowly committed to the survival and aggrandizement of their own agencies; and because these agencies, through which he must act if he is to act at all, are limited in what they can do by their predetermined routines. He doesn't so much *decide* as follow, half consciously, half blindly, the path of least resistance. Policy is not the resolution of an informed mind, but the mechanical output of a governmental machine.[1]

I cannot examine here the evidence for and against this view. I only want to suggest that, as with other scientific explanations of political action, it is very difficult to believe it. Or rather, if it were to be believed and acted upon, it would simultaneously be falsified. Imagine that the political leader, the putative decision-maker, abdicated his responsibilities under the rational agent model. "Since I cannot really decide," he says, "I will stop pretending to decide." The result of such an abdication is easy to foresee. There would be no output at all from the governmental machine. For the machine not only operates through the mind of the decision-maker; it depends upon his sense, and other people's sense, that he is actually making decisions. The (limited) options must be set out for someone to think about; the (distorted) information must be transmitted to someone's desk; the (biased) advice must be whispered in someone's ear. And what that person thinks he is doing is what we all think we are doing when we make up our minds; it is hard to imagine what else he could think and still act in the world. The rest of us could conceivably study the bureaucratic pressures to which he is subject and predict his decision. But he will hardly be satisfied to do the same. He knows that he has to *make* a decision; if he merely predicts it and does not make it, there would be no decision at all. If he were to study bureaucratic pressures, he would do so only to increase or improve his options so that he could make, if he chose, an unexpected move. Because his free decision is indispensable, he can always defeat our scientific expectations.

There are, I think, two important pictures of free deciding. I shall label them, crudely, the realist model and the moralist model, without meaning to imply that realists are not moral men and women, or that moralists are necessarily unrealistic. There are intimations of such dichotomies in our culture, not unrelated to the thrust of contemporary political science, but I don't intend to pursue them, let alone to accept them, but only to point them out.

According to the realist model, decision-making is essentially a matter of maximizing values. It involves a kind of hypothetical reasoning. If one wants x, one must do A or B or C. The value of x is generally assumed to be given, or, at any rate, beyond rational dispute; we can take national security as a paradigmatic example. Interest focuses on the means best suited to achieving that value, and the picture of how political leaders, their counselors, and their countless stand-ins decide among the alternatives is quite precisely drawn, as to both psychological tone and mental activity. First of all, the decider must be a certain sort of person. I always imagine him as a Machiavellian prince; it is, perhaps one of the more dubious achievements of democratic government that it has universalized that image. How many citizens, vicariously deciding affairs of state (how many political scientists planning a visit to Washington) preen themselves as princes—hardheaded, toughminded, cool, calculating, and ruthless! Unwavering realism is a crucial part of the image, but that should not prevent us from recognizing that the picture as a whole is a modern fantasy. Machiavelli, though he scorned idealism, was a political perfectionist. He wanted instrumental decisions to be made in an absolutely single-minded way, with regard to this question only: Which of these alternatives most efficiently (with least cost to the prince or his constituents) maximizes the value x? Decision-making is a calculation of advantage, and nothing—above all, no species of piety or sentimentality—must be allowed to interfere with the reckoning.

Even without the interference of such extraneous factors, however, the reckoning is enormously difficult. When one reflects upon these difficulties, the fantastic elements in the realist model tend to fade away; the picture is altered so as to be both more troubling and more properly realistic. The problems lie, as welfare economists have pointed out, in the arithmetic itself and not only (as Machiavelli thought) in the inhibitions of the calculators. It is difficult to specify costs and benefits for individuals and even more difficult to aggregate the results once we have arrived at some sort of specification. In practice, however, political leaders manage to do both these things, often with great confidence, as if they were easy. And once they have calculated, they drive themselves to act swiftly and decisively, without Hamlet-like hesitations and scruples. The Machiavellian model is still dominant in our culture, and I want to accept the challenge it poses and describe a second decision-making process in which the inhibitions—that is, the moral principles—of leaders and citizens figure as a major source of the decisions they make.

The difficulty with political realism is that in maximizing one value, the decision-maker is forced to curtail or override others. He does not live in a tidy world. Sometimes the conflicting values are commensurate or roughly commensurate and can be dealt with through cost/benefit analysis. But the conflict takes on an entirely different character when goal-maximizing comes up against what we conceive to be individual or collective rights. The paradigmatic case is when the pursuit of national security requires or seems to require violations of individual liberty. No doubt it is possible to contrive a kind of political arithmetic for such cases, but now the contrivance is likely to be a facade, behind which a radically different decision process is acted out. What is involved here is moral choice, and in describing moral choice, conventional realism is not a very helpful guide either to what should or to what actually does happen. Above all, it does not account for the conduct of political actors who are also, or who imagine themselves to be (who preen themselves as) moral men and women. I mean to name with that last phrase a very large group of people: all those who have moral principles and try to live by them and do the right thing, who experience moral conflicts and dilemmas, who worry about their decisions. On the realist model, decisions are calculated; on the moralist model, they are worried about. Once again, I do not want to draw a firm line. Of course, realists worry and moralists reckon, but the difference in emphasis is important.

How do moral men and women decide hard cases—cases involving individual rights, political freedom, innocent lives; cases in which deceit or violence is said by political realists to be necessary and perhaps is necessary? It is obviously not true that they will never decide to lie or to invade the sphere of privacy or even to kill innocent people. They will, sometimes, reach the same decision that realists reach, though by a different route. For they have principles which are also obstacles to the easy pursuit of goals like security and happiness. These principles cannot simply be pushed aside in the course of political calculation; they can only be overridden by some intuitive sense of direness and extremity. When they are not overridden, it is the principles that shape the policy or, at least, mark off the limits within which it can be pursued. Policy is fixed through a process of reflection upon the character and extent of individual and collective rights or, sometimes, through a recognition of present evil or looming disaster.

It is sometimes suggested that the class of moral men and women and the class of Machiavellian realists are mutually exclusive. Machiavelli himself thought that good men could rarely ("perhaps never") be found who were willing to do those bad things that are necessary to win political power and to found or reform republics.[2] This dubious proposition is widely accepted. Hence, realism tends to be seen as the attitude of the powerful and moral concern as the attitude of citizens far removed from power. Statesmen are realistic; private persons enjoy the luxury of a moral life. Or, to put the same insight in negative terms: Cynical toughmindedness is a disease that spreads outward from the center of the political system; sanctimoniousness is a disease that spreads inward from the margins.

But these distinctions are badly drawn, I think, because they fail to take into account the close resemblance of actual and vicarious decision-making in a democracy. Both models are acted out among leaders and citizens; indeed, by the same people (in both groups) at different times and by different people confronting similar issues. It is true that when our leaders draw their own portraits, they are most likely to describe themselves as princes. When they are sketched in the mass media, it is their coolness rather than their concern that we are most often asked to admire. And when we play at being leaders ourselves, realism is a constant temptation. Politics (and vicarious politics) is a school of toughness. It is important to stress, then, that in really hard cases, leaders and citizens in significant numbers act like moral men and women. That is not to say that they do the right thing, but only that they try to do the right thing. They regard individual and collective rights, human lives and liberties, with an attentiveness that is not allowed for among Machiavellian princes.

It is possible to go further than this. The recognition of hard cases already implies such an attentiveness, for the quality of "hardness" or moral difficulty is not likely to be revealed by a cost/benefit analysis. It is characteristic of political leaders who think of themselves as realists that they are disinclined to regard individual life or liberty as a significant barrier to the achievement of their purposes. In the national security versus personal liberty cases, for example, the princes among us have had little difficulty with their calculations. If we grant that there is anything at all to worry about in such cases, we are in effect making anticipative or retrospective decisions in accordance with the moralist model, and we are suggesting that actual decisions be similarly made. Now it should be the goal of political education to make that suggestion explicit and to elaborate its meaning.

Political realism is already an explicit and highly elaborated doctrine. In what are called the policy sciences, its meaning is explored, sometimes in a fantastic, sometimes in a sober and sophisticated way. Though these sciences were initially developed with policy-makers in mind as ideal students, the message filters down to the rest of us. It has become an important feature of the study of politics generally, so much so that we calculate costs and benefits almost automatically and half believe that we are natural and not socialized realists. But our moral principles and inhibitions have not been similarly legitimized by higher education. The paradoxical result is that we tend to regard them as social accessories which have to be set aside before we confront the cruel necessities of political decision-making. Fortunately, they are not easy to set aside. It would be a good thing, still, to understand them better and, above all, to understand how they function and how we function with them in the political arena. If we are educating decision-makers, we need to teach them something about moral choice.

I have taken the notion of hard cases from the law, and I shall argue later on that the education of citizens is best understood by analogy with the education of lawyers. But it will be useful first to consider a non-academic example of political education. It is not only in schools, obviously, that we learn about politics. We learn about politics *from politics*, sometimes as the subjects of political action in parties and movements, sometimes only as the objects of other people's initiatives. In either case, assuming a fairly open society, we are likely to understand what is going on and to construct a standpoint for ourselves through the processes of anticipation and retrospection that I have described.

Consider for a moment the politics of the left in the 1920s

and 1930s. It was a feature of the day-to-day life of Western communists and socialists during those years that they were focused in a peculiarly intense way on the events of the Russian revolution. That focus may not have advanced their local effectiveness, but it certainly made for an extraordinary political education—for those individuals, at least, who didn't succumb to Stalinist orthodoxy and give up the right to kibbitz. Again and again, radical activists had to ask themselves questions that were very hard to answer, and, what is equally important, they had to ask themselves the same questions and answer them within a common framework of Marxist or near-Marxist ideology. Within that framework, they quickly produced "realist" and "moralist" analyses.[3] Though Marxism as a world-historical system did not seem to invite arguments based on fundamental values and human rights, such arguments were nevertheless developed—convincing evidence, I think, of the deeply rooted and pervasive character of the moralist model.

I want to mention only one of the questions that agitated radicals during those years. I will put it in the first person singular since I have asked it of myself, though no doubt in a more detached way than it could have been asked forty or fifty years ago. Suppose that I held power in Moscow in 1921 and had to decide whether to send troops against the rebels in Kronstadt: What would I have decided? It is not a matter of making a prediction based on (probably inadequate) self-knowledge; what is called for here is a judgment. What should have been done? Historians do not commonly ask, let alone answer, questions of this sort. But it was a necessary question for all participants in the political movement or movements that had, so to speak, inherited Kronstadt and its repression. Every responsbile participant literally had to ask the question and work his way through the issues it raised: Was the security of the Bolshevik regime a value that could be maximized at any price? Or did the Bolsheviks have to recognize a right of opposition, at least among those groups they claimed to represent? Kronstadt became a kind of "case," ar-

gued and reargued in a way that suggests the casuistic character of everyday politics. One can get a sense of the importance
of the judgments called for in such cases from two articles that
Trotsky published in 1938: "Hue and Cry over Kronstadt,"
and "More on the Suppression of Kronstadt."[4] Seventeen
years after the event, it still figured significantly in radical
politics. Men and women worked out their principles or discovered what their principles really were by "deciding" what
to do about the Kronstadt rebels.

Now, different political experiences establish different sets
of cases as the necessary subject matter of retrospective judgment. I suppose that these cases can be more or less difficult
and therefore more or less educational, and so the judgments
people make can be more or less revealing of their deepest
convictions. But this sort of thing goes on all the time, not
only in leftist movements; it is a central feature of political
life. And because of its mental character, it invites imitation in
our schools.

There is one kind of academic training that already resembles the on-going casuistry of the political world.[5] The life of
the law is similarly casuistic, and students are initiated into the
legal enterprise through the study of cases. I don't mean the
analogy to be taken literally, for there are important differences between the professionalism of lawyers and the ama-
teurism of citizens. Still, there is something here that we
might find instructive.

In the judicial system, narrowly understood, judges are the
key decision-makers, while lawyers prejudge and second-
guess their decisions. Legal training prepares lawyers and
judges for this activity; it does so through a pattern of study
which was once, and perhaps still is, central also to the training of priests, but which has never been seriously proposed
for citizens. What is involved is a series of anticipative and retrospective decisions in selected historical and hypothetical
cases. Lawyers are asked to decide hard cases or to review decisions already made; they are required to go through the en-

tire process of weighing reasons and constructing arguments. They must stand on one side or another, for they are not legal scientists but future practitioners of the law. This is exactly what should be asked of citizens, for they are future political actors and real or vicarious decision-makers.

Casuistry is an educational mode more easily adapted to the study of legal decision than to the study of moral choice. For our judicial system turns out cases as a necessary artifact of its normal procedures. And it provides authoritative decisions which lawyers can reflect upon and second-guess and which then come to form the basis of their anticipative judgments. Legal principles are fleshed out as precedents; they take on a concreteness and visibility that moral principles rarely achieve.

But it would be a mistake to overemphasize the differences between morality and law. Judicial decision-making is not simply a matter of applying principles or following precedents: It requires interpretation and choice, and judges often experience the common difficulties of moral life.[6] The law does not ease these difficulties; it only provides a framework within which they can be (and have to be) resolved. The framework of morality is not so different. Though moral principles are never formulated in an official way, it is nevertheless possible at any given moment to recognize a set of principles that have, so to speak, standing in our moral world. There is, of course, no particular group of people professionally committed to these principles—as priests were committed in the days when casuistry was an established ethical science—but their binding quality is widely accepted. They figure in our moral choices in ways that are closely analogous to the role of legal principles in judicial decisions; they are a necessary reference; without them we could not choose at all.

But if principles determine decisions, decisions in turn modify and refine principles: This is the way both law and morality change over time. And in this process, it is not only authoritative decisions that count. Law school casuistry counts too, and so does vicarious decision-making generally.

The tradition of discourse to which judges refer themselves when they confront hard cases includes the anticipations and retrospections of teachers and students (as these are written up in the law reviews), as well as the opinions of previous courts. In an important sense, then, the social function of the law school is not only to teach law; it is also to make it. The case should be the same with political education at colleges and universities. Its purpose is not only to prepare future citizens for decision-making, but actually to initiate them into an ongoing process of (vicarious) decision-making. And this process, if it is really going on, is an effective way of shaping and reshaping the principles that govern decisions in the "real world." Legal education is a part of the life of the law; political education should be a part of political life.

Consider an example from international law, a legal system so radically imperfect that we often think of it simply as a moral code. In this code, there is a rule against killing prisoners of war, a rule which has its philosophical source in arguments put forward in the eighteenth century by writers like Montesquieu and Rousseau. "The object of the war being the destruction of the hostile state," wrote Rousseau, "the other side has a right to kill its defenders while they are bearing arms; but as soon as they lay them down and surrender, they cease to be enemies or instruments of the enemy, and become once more merely men, whose life no one has any right to take."[7] Now civilians and soldiers ought to understand the principles involved here, the distinction between enemies and "mere men." But that understanding will come too easily and be of little real use, to them or to the rest of us, unless they work their way through hard cases. The purpose of such an exercise is twofold: first, to turn Rousseau's general principles into rules adapted (if only in imagination) to the circumstances of actual combat, and so to shape the decisions that will actually be made; secondly, to reproduce this pattern of casuistic reflection outside the classroom, to create a certain sort of political climate. I do not mean a climate of righteousness, for in political and moral decision-making righteousness is not the most appropriate mental attitude. What we should aim at is a shared sense of moral concern. We should teach citizens to worry—or rather, we should teach them that the worrying they habitually engage in is not a sign of political naïveté and weakness. For there is no other way to make decisions in hard cases (once we have agreed that there are hard cases).

The common vice of moralists is hypocrisy; among realists it is fantasy; and in both cases we can recognize the tribute that is being paid to "virtue"—that is, to high principles and to Machiavellian single-mindedness. Now, when we convict a political leader of hypocrisy, what we actually do is to work through his decisions and claim that they were not made (could not have been made) in accordance with the principles he claims to hold. I do not want to suggest that this is a difficult enterprise; we do it all the time. The exposure of hypocrisy is one of the most common forms of retrospective decision-making—a favorite spectator sport—especially so in an age when realism is culturally dominant. The case is the same in the law. It has become a commonplace to argue that judges do not really decide cases on the basis of legal principles and precedents, but on the basis of personal political commitments and group interests. Principles and precedents, we are told, fix the form in which the decision is rendered, not the process through which it is made. No doubt, there is some truth to this view, but we have only to require students to reflect seriously on hard cases and they will see that it is a very partial truth.

Certainly, the equivalent argument in moral life is a very partial truth. Here we have, for example, an army lieutenant who professes a deep commitment to the rules of war and, above all, to the rights of prisoners of war. Recently, however, he commanded a small unit on a special mission, and his troops took several enemy soldiers captive "under such circumstances that men could not be spared to guard them . . . and that to have taken them along would have greatly endangered the success of the mission or the safety of the unit."[8]

He ordered the prisoners killed. Once we have called him a hypocrite, what do we say next? *What would we have done in his place?* In order to make a decision of that sort, we must try to grasp his reasons for his own decision. And then we must understand the force of the principle that Montesquieu and Rousseau defended. And we must choose. If we simply insist upon the principle, without considering his reasons, we are closing our eyes to the realities of war and turning morality into a kind of piety. If we tough-mindedly accept his reasons, without referring to the principle, we are denying the right of quarter and the value of innocent life—closing our eyes, I would say, to the realities of moral choice. Exposing the lieutenant's hypocrisy is not the same thing as (and is much easier than) judging his conduct. To do the latter, we must make our own decision, and that means working our way through a moral argument.

Such arguments are plausible or implausible, good or bad, right or wrong. They are subject to what might be called "ordinary moral analysis," that is, to casuistry. Casuistic reasoning is a necessary feature of actual and vicarious decision-making in hard cases. It is not an esoteric but a popular science. Nevertheless, it requires a kind of academic legitimation (not the same kind, perhaps, as the policy sciences have provided for political realism). Contemporary ethical philosophy does not often provide that legitimation; it is an enterprise carried on at too great a distance from the actualities of politics. What is needed is a combination of political theory (the study of those principles that underlie the state and that shape or should shape the conduct of its leaders) and political and social history (the study of decision-making in complex and difficult conditions). Theory is an argument about the choices we should make; history is an argument about the choices we have made. I do not doubt that these two disciplines can be put to different uses and described in grander ways, and I am not opposed to the different uses or to the grandeur. But political education has a special importance in a democracy, and we should attend to its requirements.

MICHAEL WALZER

The recognition of moral difficulty seems to me among the first of those requirements. I cannot expect that my fellow citizens, in their real and vicarious decision-making, will always make the right decisions. I can expect that they will worry about the right things. And that we can teach, as teachers of politics and history, by worrying about the right things ourselves.

What should go on in the schools is an intense and disciplined form of the anticipations and retrospections that are a normal part of democratic politics. If we could institutionalize that activity, leaders and citizens would look to the school in a new way—not only as training grounds for talented men and women, but as centers of moral argument and sources of guidance in political decision-making. I do not mean that professors of theory and history should set themselves up as moral experts or offer themselves as consultants to mayors, congressmen, cabinet members, or generals. That is not their function—or rather, they give their advice in a different way. Political and military leaders should be made aware that their moral choices are being anticipated and second-guessed in a systematic fashion. For then, inevitably, they will be drawn into the process, forced to reason according to certain standards, forced to justify their actions in certain ways. In a democracy, to educate citizens is to coerce leaders. That is the real point of teaching politics.

Politics today is an activity carried on in a state of deep moral uncertainty. We make and argue about moral choices, but we do so in a slipshod way, without confidence in the enterprise or a firm sense of its seriousness. It is impossible, of course, to be entirely ignorant of moral principles; they are a part of our common knowledge; that's why we are all kibitzers. But the triumph of elitism and realism in our political science (and our culture) has partially isolated political leaders from that common knowledge and has made anticipative and retrospective decision-making seem, even to its practitioners, an amusing and ineffectual activity. I have tried to argue that we should establish that activity on the highest intellectual level in order to give it strength and substance at every level. The moral choices that our leaders make, like legal decisions, should become the subject of systematic reflection, should be written about, discussed, and criticized. We must generate a tradition of discourse which will be, like legal discourse, unavoidable, the common and necessary reference of real and vicarious decision-makers. If we could do that, hard cases would, no doubt, remain hard, but the difficulties would be commonly recognized, and they would be resolved, like legal difficulties, in accordance with commonly accepted intellectual procedures. And though political leaders would be as lonely as ever when they made their decisions, they would at the same time, like judges, find themselves in good company. Just as there is a world of professional reference shaping the judge's decisions, generated by the anticipations and retrospections of his fellow lawyers, so there should be a world of democratic reference shaping the moral choices of our political leaders, generated by the anticipations and retrospections of their fellow citizens.

1. Graham T. Allison, *Essence of Decision* (Boston: Little Brown, 1971). Allison's argument is more subtle and complex than this crude summary can suggest. For a useful critique, see Stephen D. Krasner, "Are Bureaucracies Important? (Or Allison Wonderland)," *Foreign Policy* 7 (Summer, 1972), 159-79.

2. Niccolo Machiavelli, *The Discourses* I, 18.

3. See, for example, Leon Trotsky, *Their Morals and Ours* (New York, 1969), where Trotsky claims to set out a new Marxist ethics, but in fact defends a conventional utilitarianism against the moral absolutism of some of his opponents on the anti-Stalinist left.

4. Leon Trotsky, "The Hue and Cry over Kronstadt," and "More on the Suppression of Kronstadt," *The New International*, April 1938 and August 1938.

5. I am using the word "casuistry" here to mean (what it originally meant): "That part of Ethics which resolves cases of conscience, applying the general rules of . . . morality to particular instances which disclose special circumstances or conflicting duties" (*Oxford English Dictionary*). That casuistry in practice sometimes leads to a kind of

tinct branches. The first is analytical jurisprudence, which is meant to be the study, in more or less a philosophical way, of the principal concepts that lawyers use. These include specific legal concepts like ownership, possession, negligence, and so forth, but also the concept of law itself. What does it mean to say that a legal system exists? What does it mean to say that some proposition is a sound or correct proposition of law? The second branch of jurisprudence, on the conventional account, is sociological jurisprudence. This studies not the meaning of the terms that lawyers use, but rather the different functions of the law and the ideological presuppositions of different legal systems. Does law reflect the dominant ideologies of the culture which it helps to govern, and if so, what are the mechanics and interactions that explain this? The third branch is normative jurisprudence, and that is the study, not of what law is, but of what law should be. The traditional conception of legal philosophy insists that these three questions are different questions, and that confusion comes from trying to unite them. It is, for example, a standing objection to the legal philosophy of Professor Fuller of the Harvard Law School that he confuses a question of the analytic sort, namely the question of when a legal system exists, with a question of the normative sort, which is the question of when a legal system is a good legal system.

A second and very closely connected part of the general picture I want to expose is a theory about the point of jurisprudence so conceived. The point of asking questions about what law means, according to this theory, is not to respond to any problem that lawyers face in a professional way, but simply to satisfy the intellectual curiosity that lawyers ought to have about their discipline. Professor Hart, in the first chapter of *The Concept of Law*, presents this part of the picture very neatly. He says that lawyers are in the position of Saint Augustine who was able to tell time and keep appointments, but who fell silent when someone asked him what time is. Professor Hart thinks that lawyers are rather in that position: When you ask them whether something is the law they can say yes or no; when you ask them to argue on behalf of a client they can do that and state propositions of law in so doing; but if you ask them what *is* law, in the same querulous tone of voice you might use to ask what time is, then they fall silent. Teaching analytical jurisprudence to lawyers is, on this conception, rather like teaching watchmakers the metaphysics of time. It isn't, of course, that the watchmaker needs to be able to speculate about the nature of time in order to do an effective job of making watches, but if he is a man of ordinary intellectual curiosity, the supposition runs, then he will be maddened by the fact that he can't explain an important concept that he uses day to day. Analytical jurisprudence must be justified in the same way.

The third part of the picture, again very closely connected, is a particular assumption about what an answer to the central questions of analytical jurisprudence must be like. What is law? What does the term "law" mean? Analytical jurisprudence treats these questions as equivalent to the following question: What are the necessary and sufficient conditions for the truth of a proposition of law? By a proposition of law I mean something of this form: "The law is that you need three witnesses to a will." "The law is that capital punishment is cruel and unusual and therefore unconstitutional." Statements of this form, statements that purport to say what the law is in a particular community, are obviously very different sorts of statements from statements that assert the existence of a system of law as a political institution. There has been a certain confusion between these two questions, but they are rather easily distinguished. The statement that there was law in Nazi Germany or that there is law in one of the smaller West Indian islands is a statement of a different character from the statement that the law is that you need three witnesses to a will. The picture I am discussing assumes that the necessary and sufficient conditions for the truth of a propostion of law must be non-problematical conditions. That is, they must be conditions such that reasonable men cannot disagree, when all the facts of a case are known or stipulated, as to whether these conditions have been met. Professor Hart's theory, for example, argues that a proposition of law is an accurate or correct proposition of law just in case a rule of law from which that proposition follows has been enacted, or has developed, pursuant to a more general social rule accepted by the vast bulk of at least the legal officials in the community. The general social rule stipulates the pedigree that a more precise rule of this sort must have. If a rule requiring three witnesses to a will is part of a statute, and this statute has been enacted in conformity with the constitutive and regulative rules in a constitution, and there is in the community an almost unbroken practice among the officials of regarding what the constitution says as law, then the particular proposition embedded in the statute has been generated from the more general practice to which everyone in the community subscribes. The general social rule supplies a non-problematical set of conditions against which to test the truth of any particular proposition of law.

The fourth component of the picture I have in mind is a consequence of the others. It is a theory about how political philosophy might bear—or rather not bear—on analytical jurisprudence. It holds that the necessary and sufficient conditions for the truth of propositions of law must be matters of fact, as distinguished from matters of political morality ordinarily studied by political philosophy. If you ask questions about what the law should be, then you will find yourself asking about justice and fairness. But these questions must be carefully distinguished from the questions of analytical jurisprudence that will not drive you to political philosophy.

It follows that insofar as political philosophers and political scientists are invited to join in the work of the law school through some interdisciplinary connection, they will be invited to join what lawyers call legislative, rather than adjudicative, investigations. That is to say, they will be invited to contribute to discussions about what statutes should be enacted so as to improve the law, but they will not be invited to join discussion about how pending or puzzling law suits should be decided. By and large, the work of a law school is still heavily centered on questions of adjudication, heavily centered on the question of what courts may and should do in some novel case. Economists are more and more consulted on that very issue. But insofar as political philosophy is invited, by the paradigm I have described, to join in the enterprise, it has been asked to make its contribution on the legislative side. But that has the following consequence: The contribution that political philosophy is asked to make turns out to be a rather trivial and peripheral contribution, because the problems of legislation that are considered in law schools are for the most part problems of detail and strategy distinct from principle. They are stimulated by the fact that there is now pressing in some legislature a particular legislative program whose merits are to be examined. The level of detail at which the legislative question is asked usually means that economic considerations, for example, are likely to be much more important than questions of political theory or political philosophy.

So the general picture, which begins with some assumptions about what jurisprudence is and continues through assumptions about the right answer to certain key jurisprudential problems, has as its consequence a particular basis on which political philosophy is invited to ally itself with legal study, which insures that the contribution will not in fact be a very important or interesting one. It is hardly surprising that very few political philosophers have been anxious to accept the invitation. I want to argue that the general picture is wrong and that its central mistake lies in the assumption that the necessary and sufficient conditions for the truth of a proposition of law must be non-problematical. I shall argue, to the contrary, that there cannot be a successful non-problematical theory of what law is.

I want you to imagine the moment before an important "land mark" law suit is decided. We might take as our example the famous case called *MacPherson* v. *Buick*. That was the case in which the modern law of negligence was born in this country through an important decision by Cardozo. Mrs.

MacPherson was injured because her Buick was defective. The law at that time provided that she could sue the particular Buick dealer who had sold her the automobile. She wished to sue the Buick company itself. Opinion was divided before the case whether the manufacturers had any legal duty of that sort running directly to the ultimate purchaser. Some lawyers thought it did, and others thought not. In this famous case, Cardozo held that the Buick motor company did owe Mrs. MacPherson a duty of care, because it could foresee that negligence on its part would have consequences undesirable to her.

Now I invite you to consider the moment before the decision is announced. Cardozo's gavel is poised in mid-air. He has the text of the speech he plans to give and as the gavel is descending, the motion picture stops. Time is frozen and someone utters the proposition of law that a company in the position of the Buick motor company has the duty of care Mrs. MacPherson claims it has. It is a consequence, I take it, of any non-problematical theory about when propositions of law are true that the proposition he utters is not true. The proposition is not true simply because reasonable lawyers disagreed about the decision Cardozo should reach, and the disagreement was not simply about what some statute said or about what some other judge had said in the past about any other matter of fact. The disagreement was a disagreement about the legal consequences of what everyone agreed had happened in the institutional history of this particular case.

But roughly half of the lawyers who argued the case contended that the proposition was true before the gavel fell. Those who argued against them did not say simply that it couldn't possibly be true since reasonable lawyers disagreed about whether it was. They did not use that quick argument, but, on the contrary, produced arguments of a substantive sort. Cardozo, when the gavel fell, said by way of justifying his decision that on his understanding the law is that a manufacturer does owe such a duty of care. In other words, all the parties to the argument and to its solution assumed either the truth of the proposition or at least the possible truth of the proposition. They were united in assuming that it was not obviously not true, and yet it is a consequence of any non-problematical theory that it cannot be true.

The following reply will be made by anyone who wishes to defend such a theory. Though lawyers in a controversial case will say that the law is such and such, though the judge in giving his opinion will often give that as his justification for reaching the decision he does, they don't mean that at all. They mean something else, namely that the law ought to be what they say it is. Their statement that it already is the law is a mendacious but harmless convention like the English convention of wearing a wig.

That seems to me a wholly unsuccessful translation of what lawyers mean to say when they say the law is such and such before the gavel has come down in a novel decision. But I don't want to press that point, because even if it were an illuminating translation it would still not be a satisfactory reply to the objection I made. It is not enough to say that in such a case lawyers mean to make claims about what the law ought to be, because that explanation fails to take account of an important distinction. It must be conceded by anyone who takes this line that lawyers then talk about what the law ought to be in two very different senses. In the first of these senses (which I shall call "ought-plus") it means the law ought to be that someone in the position of Mrs. MacPherson can recover against the Buick Company *and it is the duty or responsibility of the court so to decide.* Sometimes lawyers want to say something very different, which we might call "ought-minus." That is that the law ought to be (perhaps) that someone in the position of Mrs. MacPherson should recover, but if the law is to be that, then it lies to the legislature or some other body to change the law, because as things now stand the law is *not* what it ought to be. In other words, the distinction that I press upon you is a distinction between claims about what the law ought to be that are presented as reasons for a decision in favor of the plaintiff and as reasons *against* such a decision. It

RONALD DWORKIN

cannot be thought that when lawyers say that the law is such and such in a controversial case, they mean to say only that this is what the law ought-minus to be.

If we accept the suggested translation, then we must recognize that there are at least three sorts of propositions that must be accounted for by any satisfactory theory about the necessary and sufficient conditions for the truth of propositions of law. One is a non-problematical statement that the law is such and such. The second is a statement about what the law ought-plus to be, and the third is a statement about what the law ought-minus to be. If we accept that series of possible statements, then the important distinction for a theory of law is not between the first and the second but between the first two and the third. I might pause to notice that if you suppose that the point of analytical jurisprudence is to deal with questions that appeal to one's intellectual curiosity, like the question of what time is, then this might not to you a particularly troubling point. That is, you might say that you can raise all of the interesting philosophical questions, like questions about what rules are, just in treating the first of these three types of propositions. If, on the other hand, you take the opposite view, which I hold, namely that the point of analytical jurisprudence is to deal just with the troublesome cases that press our conceptions of what law is and demand that we refine them, then the failure to speak to this second class of questions, once the three are distinguished, is culpable. Indeed it trivializes the theory, because the theory then stops exactly at the point where the intellectual demands on the theory begin.

What might be now said by a defender of the argument that an interesting non-problematical account can be given of propositions? He might say that in fact no set of necessary and sufficient conditions can be given for ought-plus statements of law. But what does that mean? It might mean at least two different things. First, it might mean that no *non-problematical* analysis can be given for ought-plus statements, which of course is true. But the whole point of my objection is just to challenge the idea that the only proper analysis of law is a set of non-problematical conditions. Second, it might mean that any attempted analysis would be open to counter-examples. Counter-examples, however, must be understood to be of a certain form in order to be troubling to a *problematical* analysis. The claim that a non-problematical analysis makes is the claim that reasonable men will always agree as to when the conditions it stipulates have been met. That is not the claim of a problematical theory. Therefore it does not refute a problematical theory simply to present a case in which reasonable men disagree as to whether the conditions are met. It is necessary to produce cases in which lawyers do agree that the conditions are met, but disagree nevertheless whether the proposition of law attached to these conditions is true. That would indeed be a counter-example. It seems, therefore, that the most interesting claim made by a non-problematical theory of law, at least the claim that most immediately bears on the subject of the connection between political philosophy and analytical jurisprudence, is just the claim that no analysis of ought-plus propositions of law can be given which does not suffer from counter-examples of that serious form.

I think such an analysis can be given. The rough form of the analysis I have in mind would be this: Suppose we have an adequate non-problematical theory of law, like Hart's theory, that sets out *sufficient* conditions for the truth of any propositions of law. Collect together all of the propositions which at any particular time are true propositions of law by virtue of this non-problematical theory. Find for that vast collection of rules and principles of law the political theory that offers the best justification of the entire collection. What political theory would provide the best justification for enacting just that set of rules? That political theory would be terribly complex. It would have very abstract levels to justify constitutional arrangements and more detailed levels which justify rules of civil and criminal law. It would contain both principles (by which I mean propositions asserting individual rights) and policies (by which I mean propositions deploying collective goals of the community). It would have all of this. You will, of course, appreciate that there might be more than one political theory that could furnish some sort of a justification of any particular set of rules. The best justification would be better than other justifications on either or both of two dimensions. It might be a better fit, accounting more satisfactorily for the detail of the rules, or it might be politically sounder, coming closer to a description of the rights that people actually do have and the collective goals that the community in fact ought to pursue.

The second dimension, of course, is a normative dimension. It is the feature of this analysis which insures that the analysis is a problematical rather than a non-problematical analysis. The analysis supposes that particular propositions of law entailed by the principles of the best justification (not the policies but the principles) are themselves true propositions of law. So the analysis argues that there are two ways in which a proposition of law can be defended. One might argue that it meets the non-problematical tests, which are sufficient conditions, or that it follows from the assumptions about individual rights that are necessary to provide the best justification of those settled rules of law. Obviously, a great deal more that must be said in order to make such a theory even precise enough to ask whether there is much to say in its favor. I have tried to do this elsewhere,[2] and won't repeat the arguments now because I want to ask this different question.

Suppose this problematical theory were to replace the non-problematical theories now in fashion. It would generate a picture of the connection between political philosophy and legal studies that would be different in each of the particulars I distinguished. In the first place, there could no longer be a sharp distinction between fact and value in this area. There could no longer be a sharp distinction between the question of what in detail the law is and what it ought to be. The theory proposes a connection between law and morality explicated by this notion of the best justification that can be given to the law, however wicked it might be, that we now have. To begin to specify what is in fact the best justification of a particular legal system is to begin to answer the analytical question and the normative question at the same time.

If the theory that I have offered were accepted, the contribution that political philosophy would be asked make to problems of adjudication would be much more significant than the contribution it can make to the legislative questions to which it is remitted by the earlier analysis. Why? Because questions of adjudication are entirely and systematically questions of principle. They are questions minimally diluted by considerations of the detail of political practice, or of economic affairs, which make consideration of legislative questions at the law school level an appropriate medium for political philosophy. Once political philosophers are invited to participate at the right level, I should think the invitation would be difficult to resist.

I'll close with two examples of problems of adjudication which cry out for the attention of political philosophers. Many of you are familiar with Ronald Coase's important article, "The Problem of Social Cost," in which he discusses cases like the famous old English case of *Sturges* v. *Bridgeman*.[3] A doctor in Wigmore Street had a consulting room he rarely used, which adjoined a candymaker's shop. He began one day to use the consulting room for the specific purpose of trying out the new invention of the stethoscope. He found that he got very insecure reports from the stethoscope because there was, next to this room, in the confectionary, a crystal-cracking machine that beat with a different rhythm, and so he sued in the High Court of Justice for relief. You might think the case raised the question of whether it was fair that the doctor should be inconvenienced in that way. Coase and others have argued at great length that cases of this sort neither are nor should be decided on grounds of fairness at all. We should not ask whether it is fairer to make the confectionary give up its business. We should look ahead and ask whether society will gain more on the whole, in economic efficiency, by requiring one or the other party to withdraw.

This is an unappealing way to look at these questions, it seems to me, and I am prepared to argue that it is an almost incoherent way. But it does open a problem which I think is a problem for political philosophy. Coase and the others have shown that the decisions judges reach in these cases are the decisions they would reach if they were concerned with economic efficiency rather than fairness. Suppose we accept that cases in this area can be *explained* by the doctrine of economic efficiency in the sense that the doctrine fits, but we cannot accept that this doctrine of economic efficiency offers a *justification* for the decisions. Then this question is left. Can we discover and defend a theory of individual rights that is extensionally equivalent to the requirements of efficiency because it makes the social consequences of what the doctor or candymaker does relevant to their moral rights in the way these cases seem to assume?

The second problem I have in mind is raised by Supreme Court cases testing the requirements of the Equal Protection Clause. Doctrine in this area stands, from a lawyer's standpoint, in an absolutely deplorable condition. On the one hand it is said that sensible government must make distinctions that are to a considerable degree arbitrary from a moral point of view. Legislatures must be free to treat groups differently for the purpose of serving adequately the needs of society, and it is ridiculous to suppose that a government can pursue its social responsibilities without administrative classifications that injures some as against others. In a famous case the Supreme Court had to decide whether the rule that oculists but not opticians could prescribe glasses was fair. The Court said the government must get on and made distinctions and that the court can't be a place where people who happen to fall on the wrong side of lines come to cry. On the other hand, there is a disposition to say that certain classifications among welfare recipients, are inherently unjust and unconstitutional. There has thus far been produced no general theory of equality that explains why the one decision but not the other is a denial of equality. Lawyers try to explain the distinction by saying that

in some cases the classification is inherently suspect and must
be subject to special scrutiny, whereas in other cases the classification is not suspect and therefore need not be subject to
scrutiny. There is a marvelous failure, however, to describe
what this suspicion is a suspicion of and what the special
scrutiny is meant to discover. It is thought to be enough to
say that there must be special scrutiny and that the classification is suspicious. What is desperately needed in this area is a
theory of equality that does two things: It must explain the
run of Supreme Court decisions, and it must do this in the
form of an independently appealing conception of equality
that we can inspect for its political morality and philosophical
coherence. That is not simply a job that political philosophers
might assist lawyers in doing; it is a job that no one else can
do.

1. This is an edited transcript of remarks at the conference. Several
of the points made here are developed in Ronald Dworkin, *Taking
Rights Seriously* (Cambridge, Mass.: Harvard University Press,
1977).

2. See Chapter 4 of *Taking Rights Seriously*.

3. Ronald Coase, "The Problem of Social Cost," *Journal of Law
and Economics*, 3 (1960), 19-28.

POLITICAL THEORY AND POLITICAL COMMENTARY

SHELDON WOLIN

The problems addressed in this paper are two: the interrelations between political theory and political commentary and their differences. The approach to these problems will be to consider political theory and political commentary as definite, even highly stylized, modes of activity. Both are concerned with the interpretation of politics and both engage in interpretation in a political way. Theory and commentary, it will be contended, are not only about politics; they are politics expressed through the act of interpretation. The paper, then, is about the politics of interpretation.

In exploring the subject I shall be using a severe conception of political theory and theoretical activity based on the examples of the great writers whose works have served to constitute the Western tradition of political theory, e.g., Plato, Aristotle, Machiavelli, Hobbes, Locke, Marx, etc. This might appear to be an arbitrary choice, but it has the advantage of helping us to locate the element of commentary within a political theory, as well as to distinguish it from a form of commentary which is theoretical but not resident within a theory. The theories of the writers mentioned previously all contain commentaries upon politics, not simply upon politics in general, but upon contemporary institutions, leaders, and events, as well as upon past politics. In Plato, for example, we can find an interpretation of contemporary Athenian politics as well as of the Periclean politics of an earlier generation; in Machiavelli, a commentary upon Florentine politics and upon the politics of ancient Rome.

There is another and more recent form of commentary by
political theorists, one which is not literally embodied in a
theory. Roughly speaking, from about the seventeenth century to the present, political theorists have used other and
more popular media in order to comment upon politics.
Writers such as Harrington, Locke, and Burke wrote pamphlets; Hegel, Marx, John Stuart Mill, Tocqueville, and Max
Weber used the medium of newspapers or magazines to deliver their views on politics. In availing himself of these means
of expression, the theorist would seem to have exchanged
roles. He has become, at least temporarily, a political commentator. He will have moved from the more certain realm of
theoretical controversy and discussion to a less predictable,
more public realm of politics. Instead of submitting his ideas
to a small group of fellow-theorists, he will be exposing them
to a diverse and unknown audience. Like the citizen of Rousseau's *Social Contract*, who undergoes a dramatic transformation when he becomes a member of civil society, some theorists, when they turn to commentary, have likewise displayed
evidence of transformation, at least in style. The newspaper
articles by Hegel and Weber display a refreshing vigor and di-
rectness not found in their formal writings. Commentary has
allowed them to be more uninhibitedly political. When the
theorist becomes a commentator, he is no longer required to
sublimate his political commitments in the symbolic form of
a theory. To use the example of Weber again, instead of expressing vicariously his conception of heroic action in the por-
trait of the early Protestant capitalist, he will engage the powers of the world himself, attacking the trivialization of politics
which he found rampant in the ruling circles of his day.

The example of Weber is also cautionary. The continuity
which united his theoretical preoccupations with his political
commentaries is a reminder that the theorist-turned-com-
mentator has not shed his theoretical view. Rather, he has
used the theory to inform his commentary and he has made of
commentary an intimation of his theory. Commentary becomes the attempt to entice the reader, to draw him out of

one way of looking at politics in order to attract him toward another and different way. The essential element of the activity and its political quality are contained in the phrase "a way of looking at politics" or, more succinctly, in the word "looking." The aim of the theorist is to use commentary as the means for changing the political perceptions of his readers. He wants to alter the accepted ways of viewing politics, to change the familiar appearance of politics. As commentator, the theorist is engaged in the politics of perception.

The concept of perception is crucial because of the unique opportunity offered by political commentary. By virtue of other influences to which the reader has been exposed, his attention has been directed to visual objects in the public world. Newspapers, magazines, movies, radio, and television have created vivid representations of "reality" and striking imagery, the pictorialization of politics which has accustomed the reader or viewer to "see." Even the written word of the newspaper or the spoken word of radio seek to evoke picture-like impressions in the mind of the reader or listener. The aim of these and other media is not primarily to give a report or account of political events and actions, but to create the impression among viewers, readers, or listeners that they are seeing events materialize and actions personified. As a result, the task of the political theorist engaged in commentary is greatly simplified. He may never know what has been the firsthand political experience of the members of his audience, but he can learn about their secondhand experience by observing the pictures and images infesting the public world created by the media. This makes it possible for him to estimate where they are "at" and where he might begin the task of moving them to a different *view*-point. In this connection, we might recall that Plato's dialogues typically begin with a question about everyday experience and familiar appraisals of it. Common experience remains the starting point for today's theorist. The difference is that the contemporary theorist must address an audience whose common experience of politics is mostly secondhand, which is to say that the problem does not lie in the quality of the shared experiences, but in the quality (and quantity) of the shared interpretations of filtered or pre-digested experience. It is the nature of the contemporary world that most politics, especially the politics that controls the main direction of our lives, is rarely experienced and perceived directly. Our political preferences must necessarily be expressed as preferences for some interpretations over others. This means that there is a politics taking place among those engaged in interpretation.

Before discussing the politics of interpretation, I want to point out that there is an implication to my last remarks which can serve to prepare the way for that discussion. The political importance I wish to assign to interpretation has a decisive bearing upon the kind of politics with which the theorist is concerned when he is doing commentary. The common understanding of politics is that it consists of policy questions or issues, e.g., alternative energy sources, the desirability of oil depletion allowances, or military aid to Cambodia. In this view, politics is presented in the form of a choice to be made between available means. If one were to undertake to track down the course of this view, that is, to inquire why it is that this has become the dominant view of politics, one would encounter another form of interpretation that reduces politics to a choice between means. The most obvious example is the economist's method of reducing politics to choices that have been fashioned according to criteria of economic reasoning.

If one were persuaded that, in principle, all politics could be reduced to choices of this kind, it would follow that all political commentary should be conducted by specialists or—to the extent that choices in specialized areas, such as foreign policy, defense, and environmental protection, can be translated into economic choices—primarily by economists. If, on the other hand, one is persuaded that the policy form of politics is constituted by a prior act of interpretation, then political commentary's primary concern is not to weigh choices but to contest meanings. In this latter view, policy questions are signifiers and the task of commentary is to explore what is being signified.

Whatever shortages our society may be suffering from today, it does not lack for political commentary. Judging from the amount of commentary available in newspapers, magazines, reviews, journals, television, and radio, the art is alive and flourishing. Although this allows for the expression of a rather wide range of opinions, the diversity of viewpoints seems less significant than the preeminence of a small number of commentators, such as the columnists associated with the great national newspapers or the commentators who appear on the national television networks. They are indisputably the masters and style-setters of political commentary. Without intending it to sound envious or to be a disguised plea for affirmative action, none of the well-established commentators considers himself to be a political theorist, and it is not surprising, therefore, that the most familiar forms of political commentary are untheoretical. This practice of political commentary can be summarized as the analysis or examination of current public events, personages, institutions, policies, or problems which issues in an informed observation or interpretation. Needless to say, the commentary may be critical or supportive, or some combination of the two.

Like most definitions, this one is not particularly illuminating. At best it supplies us with some rough clues about the activity of political commentary. But we want to know how we should go about the task of understanding this theoretically unself-conscious form. Should we consider it to be an autonomous activity, governed by conventions peculiar to itself, a guild perhaps? Or is it a dependent activity responsive to or controlled by external influences? Or does it lie somewhere in between?

These questions suggest that political commentary presents us with a problem of interpretation, or, more precisely, a problem of political interpretation. The political meaning of commentary arises as a problem because the activity has become institutionalized, which is to say that it is not only situated within certain structures of influence and control, but that it performs certain functions on their behalf. This means, among other things, that the interpretative role of this (untheoretical) form of political commentary will have special features which, as I shall try to suggest subsequently, contrast sharply with those identified with the theoretical form of commentary.

It does not require elaborate research to identify the location of the major political commentators. They are lodged within the great structure of the media industry, which is itself a part of the political economy of our corporationist society. The main elements of that political economy are governmental bureaucracies and large-scale economic enterprises. Its politics is primarily concerned with adjusting relationships between the two main elements, each of which is exposed to numerous pressures.

In a general sense, the activity of political commentary is a function of its location. Crudely stated, its function is to interpret the system so as to render its nature unproblematic. There are primarily two ways that political commentary goes about its appointed task. The first finds the commentator involved in political education. He uses commentary as a way of initiating his reader-citizen into a way of thinking about and responding to current issues. By the issues he selects and the form in which he presents them, the commentator projects a version of politics and a version of the good citizen. One commentator may seek to convey a picture of politics as a series of difficulties with which decent and reasonably honorable men are trying to cope as best they can; the citizen should, therefore, adopt complementary attitudes: He should be reasonable, mindful of the burdens borne by public men, and respectful of the dignity of public office. Another commentator may depict politics as a series of obscenities which requires a citizen to be sardonic and cynical if he is to take the spectacle at all seriously. Without attempting to catalogue the possible variations on these themes, the main purpose of this form of political education can be understood only within the larger context of a society in which citizens are essentially powerless. Within that larger context, political education by commentary is not intended to galvanize the citizenry into action but to keep it gently oscillating between resignation and hope. Commentary accomplishes this by purveying an illusion that when the citizen reads or listens to a commentary, he is deliberating about politics. He is encouraged to believe that he is being asked to make up his mind on an issue or to indicate his policy preference. Among the functions of commentary one of the most important is to establish limits beyond which deliberation ought not to stray. For the commentator, politics is typically the art of the possible within the limits set by the existing political economy. His task is not to combat the unthinkable, but to avoid the unutterable.

That political commentary should take this form has little to do with the political preferences of particular commentators and nothing at all to do with moral rectitude. It is, instead, related to another role assumed by the commentator. He is not only a political educator to the citizens, but something of a counselor to the politicians he writes about, mingles among, and, to some extent, relies upon for information. Political commentary is full of advice, criticisms, warnings, and encouragements intended for the eyes and ears of those who rule; or at least for those who occupy high office in the government. Despite the fact that the humblest citizen is aware of the political influence exercised by those who man our economic institutions, they are rarely the subject or object of political commentary, unless they happen to be trade union leaders. For what seem like obvious reasons, most political commentators are reluctant to treat our society as a political economy.

By way of summarizing, I should like to return to an assertion advanced earlier in this paper. The function of political commentary, I suggested, is to interpret the system so as to render its nature unproblematic. This is done by largely accepting the policy-maker's definition of the "problem" and then commenting upon it. Even though the commentator may criticize an action or a proposal, he remains confined within a political world constituted by actors and policy-makers. The world presents him with endless "problems" which encourage political discourse to become identified with political "debate" about issues; it does not present him with a question about the constitution of the political world itself, because that might jeopardize the terms on which the system is interpretable.

When seen in this way, political commentary reveals itself to be a particular kind of interpretation, one that comments on politics in the way that one would expound a received text. The system is the analogue to the text. The institutions, laws, usages, and practices of the system represent the exegetical principles that give meaning to it. Policy questions and issues stand for "problems," which have to be reconciled with the accepted meaning of the text. The text itself must not be allowed to be viewed as problematic, that is, to require for its understanding a principle which casts doubt on the whole. Given the status of the text in this form of interpretation, it is easy to understand why political commentary can proceed without a theory. The text of society in its official version is the theory.

The Watergate "problem" supplies an example of how a "text" can furnish rules of interpretation for making sense out of a troubled situation. When the Watergate break-in was first publicized, the common interpretation was to treat it as merely another instance of the trickery incidental to normal "politics." Then, as more and more "facts" were uncovered, the circles of complicity became wider, another category of interpretation was utilized: Watergate was a "scandal" involving laundered money, illegal payments, and political favors. Finally, when the responsibility of the President became undeniable, legal categories of impeachment and conspiracy were introduced in order to confine the meaning of Watergate to proportions consistent with the perpetuation of the existing political system.

Two principles were given special emphasis throughout the Watergate controversy. Both are of enduring significance in the history of American self-interpretation. The first is that politics is essentially a matter of deals, of bargains struck; the second is that the American political system is to be understood as a constitutional government in which the legal "rules of the game" are controlling over the actions of the players. The two principles were invoked at different phases of the Watergate affair to signify that certain actions were to be understood as having "gone too far" by one or the other principle. The importance of these principles is not only that they furnish "standards" of legitimate behavior, but also categories which constitute the facts in such a way as to promote a particular mode of interpretation. When the Watergate activities were successively treated as "dirty tricks," violations of the laws governing campaign contributions, or, finally, as "high crimes and misdemeanors," the effect was to assign the activities to the status of "problems," that is, to being isolated aberrations which could be handled by restoring, rather than changing, fundamental arrangements (e.g., tightening the regulations concerning campaign contributions, rather than altering the conditions of politics which entail dependence on big donors).

"Distance to things and men," Max Weber once wrote, is a crucial quality for the political actor, and lack of it "is one of the deadly sins of every politician." Distance was also the quality which Weber tried to cultivate in his own theoretical investigations. Indeed, it is not too much to say that, in recommending that quality to politicians, Weber was attempting to transfer to political activity a virtue characteristically associated with theoretic activity. Ever since Plato first established his Academy on the outskirts of Athens, away from the bustling political life of the *agora*, distance has figured as a persistent element in the practice of theory. It has signified the importance of being removed from politics in order to see into it more clearly, of establishing not only space between politics and the theorist but a different order of time for putting the present and the emerging future into "perspective."

The perfect account of the theorist's quest for distance can be found near the end of Tocqueville's chapter on "The Present and Probable Future Condition of the Three Races" in the United States:

> My present objective is to embrace the whole from one point of view; the remarks I shall make will be less detailed, but they will be more sure. I shall perceive each object less distinctly, but I shall outline the principal facts with more certainty. A traveler who has just left a vast city climbs the neighboring hill; as he goes farther off, he loses sight of the men he has just quitted; their dwellings are confused in a dense mass; he can no longer distinguish the public squares and can scarcely trace out the great thoroughfares; but his eye has less difficulty in following the boundaries of the city, and for the first time he sees the shape of the whole.[1]

As Tocqueville's formulation suggests, distance has to do with the theorist's location, and location, as we have noted earlier, is one of the conditioning factors shaping much of contemporary political commentary of the a-theoretical type. The latter stands in close proximity to politics — the "Washington commentator" is the symbol of this — and he "sees" a great deal of politics firsthand; and yet he seems to "see" very little. He lacks distance, but it is not because, physically, he is too close to events. Rather, his problem is that the events or actions he is analyzing are part of the "text" composed of the prevailing understandings and practices he takes for granted. In this connection, the political function of the "text" is to provide a "covering" principle for assimilating new problems so that they appear familiar, even though perplexing or difficult. The precise purpose of a "text" is to furnish *context* rather than distance.

Theoretical activity establishes distance by means of the theory, not by choice of residence. Theory does not provide a text to which the "problems" of existing politics can be referred, but a form of criticism in which the "text" itself becomes a problem and existing politics problematic. The distance it establishes is a critical distance, a distance that renders familiar occurrences strange. The underlying purpose is not to criticize particular issues or to take sides in a debate over policies, but to expose hidden and troubling interconnections that call into question the authority of the "text."

What must the practical world be like for theoretic activity of this kind to be possible? Why, instead of simply generating "problems," does a political society develop into something problematic? An answer that will allow us to expand our notions about political-theory-as-commentary might run like this: Every political society makes distinguishing claims about itself and these it presents as its principles. It may claim, for example, to be a "free society" which respects the rights of its members to think, act, and believe as they wish, subject only to certain minimal restraints. Or it may claim to be a "welfare society" which guarantees the fulfillment of certain basic economic and social needs of its citizens. Or it may claim even more, to be an equalitarian society in which all citizens will be required to work, no individual or class will own the basic resources and social instrumentalities, and all will receive roughly comparable rewards.

These principles, together with their implementing practices, provide coherence to a society and enable it to define itself to itself and to the outside world. There is, however, a catch. No matter how generously drawn, every set of principles is exclusionary, by design as well as by operation. *Determinatio est negatio*, as Spinoza noted. A small example would be the prohibition of Article I, section 9, of the American Constitution against titles of nobility; a large example would be Article I, section 2, which describes how slaves were to be counted in the apportionment of representation and taxation. While any principle tends to be exclusionary, the historical

circumstances under which political principles are established
serve to enhance that quality. Some of the most famous political principles have been enunciated to define a new revolutionary régime and its contrast with the preceding régimes.
Political principles are usually established in opposition to
other principles and to the groups identified with them. Principles, in short, are intended to exclude. By the same token,
they also favor some groups over others, even when the principle purports to apply to all citizens. Not all citizens or
groups can avail themselves of the benefits or protections of
the principles. A fair trial means little to the person who cannot pay for a lawyer; a taxation code does not apply equally if
some citizens can purchase an accountant.

Although discrimination is built into the principles of a system, most systems, or their spokesmen, are shy about defining the system as one which promotes, for example, injustice
as well as justice, inequality as well as equality, slavery as well
as freedom. Thus the Preamble to the American Constitution
boasts to all the world of a new order dedicated to "justice"
and to securing "the blessings of liberty"; but the same doc-
ument averts its eyes, so to speak, when it provides for the
perpetuation of the slave trade (I,9): Slaves are described
euphemistically as "persons" and the whole embarrassing
business is thankfully transferred to the jurisdiction of the
states. The excluded groups, interests, and values form a "secret history," subsisting within the society but not officially
of it. Depending on the dynamics of a society, the elements of
the secret history may increase or their composition change. It
is not only oppressed racial or religious minorities, or a social
class that count as excluded elements. Cultural values and
even whole styles of politics and political action may likewise
be relegated to the margins of society. Plato protested against
the exclusion of philosophers from politics, Tocqueville
against democracy's suspicion of the man of surpassing political ability and ambition. The point is that the principles by
which a society defines itself, the principles which constitute a
"text," are not a description of actuality, a textbook, even

though the society must pretend that that is the case. Potentially, every society embodies "secret" principles which cannot be publicly professed or treated as part of the "text" because they are the source of anomalies or manifest evils which the society wants to deny, conceal, or explain away.

The coexistence of two conflicting interpretive principles, which signify two coexisting and interdependent conditions, establishes the conditions in which political theory is possible. This is what Marx meant when he wrote, "All science would be superfluous if the outward appearance and the essence of things directly coincided." For the political theorist, outward appearances need explaining because of what they suppress. The two are interconnected, but the principles that connect them are not the principles from which it is claimed that the outward appearances are derived. The principles that explain the outward appearances or official conception of reality are to be sought elsewhere, in a reality that escapes the categories which have been fashioned to make the everyday world appear familiar and acceptable. Marx gives a useful formulation of this, although the same point is to be found in different versions in the writings of earlier theorists.

> It is always the direct relationship of the owners of the conditions of production to the direct producers . . . which reveals the innermost secret, the hidden basis of the entire social structure, and with it the political form of the relation of sovereignty and dependence, in short, the corresponding specific form of the state.[2]

The function of the critical principle is to expose unsuspected interconnections in society, especially between the features which are taken for granted or as matters of pride and those which are cause for shame. In revealing the interconnections, the theorist is contending that the two "sides" form a whole and that truthfulness requires that we face up to both sides. Because of the critical principle embodied in the workings of society, the evil or shameful consequences are part of the normal operation of the system.

A political theory is not only a critical vision of existence, but a glimpse of reality, of a better social order, of a more authentic life. To view it as the "utopian element" in theory is to distort its origins. The theorist's vision of a better political order and new civic culture draws its understanding from the critical portion of the theory. The vision is complementary to the critique. And this is why political commentary is not an unnatural act for a theorist but a necessity. Political commentary is political theory conducted by other means. For the theorist it is a salutary form of self-criticism that compels him to the test of whether his ideas can make some sense of the world around him. But beyond the problem of personal development, there is his public task of political education. This task, I have tried to suggest, centers around political perception. Its purpose is to draw citizens into seeing familiar phenomena differently, as a part of a more extended tracery, as part of a problematic. Political commentary, then, can serve not only as an extension of theory but a justification of it as an activity.

1. Alexis de Tocqueville, *Democracy in America*, tr. Phillips Bradley, 2 vols. (New York: Vintage Books, 1945), I, 429.

2. Karl Marx, *Capital*, 3 vols. (New York: International Publishers, 1967), III, 817.